Relapse Prevention Counseling for
African Americans:

A Culturally Specific Model

Relapse Prevention Counseling for African Americans:
A Culturally Specific Model

By
Roland Williams
and
Terence T. Gorski

Based on the CENAPS Model of Treatment

Herald House/Independence Press
Independence, Missouri

Additional copies of this book and other addictions resources based on the CENAPS Model of Treatment can be obtained through the publisher:

Herald House/Independence Press
3225 South Noland Road
P.O. Box 1770
Independence, MO 64055-0770
Telephone: 1-800-767-8181 or 816/252-5010
Fax: 816/252-3976
Internet Web Page: http://www.heraldhouse.org
E-mail: hhmark@heraldhouse.org

ISBN-0-8309-0774-2
Printed in the United States of America

01   00   99   98   97   1   2   3   4   5

Table of Contents

Acknowledgments

This book is the result of many minds, hearts, and souls. Several friends, family members, and colleagues have made some contribution. Their love, encouragement, and direction helped me to clarify my thoughts and write a better book. This page is a chance for me to express my deep gratitude to you all.

First, I would like to thank God, for blessing me with an appreciation for recovery, a vision, and another chance.

I would like to thank and acknowledge the members of my advisory committee; these men spent many hours providing valuable feedback and support as this work unfolded. They are all experts in the field, and this work would not have been possible without them. Much love to you all.

- Thomas Fentress, CAS, senior counselor for ESO Steps, San Jose, California.
- George Jurand, pre-release administrator, Northern California Service League, San Francisco, California.
- Jamal Bey, prevention services coordinator, Brothers Network, San Francisco, California.
- Calvin Cregg Johnson, ACRPS, coordinator, Roads to Recovery, Northern California Service League, San Francisco, California.
- Mel "L.B." Turnbough, coordinator, Harriman Jones Medical Group, Long Beach, California.
- Kenny Hall, CAS, executive director, Black Eyes Productions, San Jose, California.
- Carl B. Skinner, senior counselor, Swords to Plowshares, Veterans Advocacy Organization, San Francisco, California.

Thank you to all the brothers and sisters who took time to answer the survey.

A special thanks to the following people who supported the project through their time, effort, enthusiasm, and critique:

- Charles Vincent, M.D.
- Luther Brock Sr.
- The staff at Free at Last in East Palo Alto, California, especially Lynne White and Prya Haji
- The following CENAPS faculty who offered free editing and lots of support: Kirsten Shields, Vincent A. Froehlich, Bill Eckles, and Mary Jane Saksa

Special thanks to my "little sisters": Barbara Jeanrenaud and Beth Simms—two angels for sure. Elga Torres and Jackie Mikkelsen, you're both blessings in my life. My best friend Rick Glendon, who watches my back, to Chuck Norman, who continues to show me what recovery really means, and to Richard Lindsey who inspired me to work with others.

Thanks to my five-year-old son Nicholas who accidentally pulled the plug on my computer, forcing me to examine a few of my own relapse warning signs and giving me the opportunity to redo and rethink much of this work. I love you, Bubba. To my wife Nanette and son Ramone, your love fills me up and gives me something to look forward to each day.

And a most special thanks to Terry and Carmela Gorski. Terry, without you there would be no CRPSs. Relapse prevention would still be in the Stone Age. Thanks for all the guidance, confidence, and direction. And most of all, thanks for encouraging me to make this a better book. Carmela, CENAPS would not be what it is today if it weren't for you—you make a difference. Thanks and much love to you both.

Roland Williams

Foreword

By Terence T. Gorski
President, The CENAPS Corporation

The book *Relapse Prevention Counseling* by Roland Williams represents the first major effort to adapt the CENAPS Model of Recovery and Relapse to the specific cultural needs of African Americans. I am confident that this book reflects, in a general way, a number of special obstacles faced by African Americans that are not experienced by members of the majority culture who seek recovery.

The CENAPS Model is intentionally designed to be as culturally neutral as possible. Certified Relapse Prevention Specialists are trained in methods for making cultural translations as the warning signs are personalized and analyzed. Over the years many counselors who work extensively with African Americans have identified, in a general way, a collection of warning signs that are unique to African Americans. These counselors have reported that when these culturally specific high-risk situations and relapse warning signs are translated into language that their clients understand, more clients are able to avoid relapse. The Relapse Prevention Specialists who have done this cultural translating report that their patients benefit by identifying issues related to relapse that would not have been identified had the specific cultural context been ignored.

In reading this book it is important to remember three things. First, there is great diversity in the African-American community. There is no one, single African-American culture. As a result there is no one, universal set of African-American relapse warning signs. There do, however, seem to be some common themes related to the black experience in America that create special problems for a significant number of African Americans in recovery. If these issues are identified and matched with appropriate coping strategies it is possible that many African Americans who now consider themselves hopeless may find the key that will open the lock that shuts them out of long-term recovery.

Second, African Americans represent only one of many cultural minorities in the United States. Many of these other minority cultures may benefit from reading about the specific African- American relapse warning signs. Hopefully this work will prompt others to develop culturally-specific relapse warning signs.

Third, a minority culture is always defined in relationship to the majority culture. A person does not understand the issues related to discrimination until and unless they find themselves as a minority in a majority culture. It is easy for members of the majority culture to look superficially at minority cultures and say that discrimination does not exist. It is not helpful to minimize or deny that there are special issues that block initial entry into recovery and that often lead to dropping out of recovery and into relapse.

I am pleased and honored that Roland Williams agreed to undertake this first step in what I hope will be a major initiative in understanding and becoming more effective at identifying and managing the culturally-specific issues that lead to relapse.

Introduction

This is a book about culture, chemical dependency recovery, and relapse prevention. I will focus primarily on African-American issues, but the format is such that it can be used working with any minority population. I will share some informal statistics that are the result of a nonscientific, informed survey. However, they do illustrate the need for a culturally sensitive approach to treatment and relapse prevention. I will introduce Relapse Warning Signs for African Americans. These are twenty-two warning signs that might surface, in addition, to the warning signs experienced by every other addict/alcoholic. I have attempted to illustrate several issues that have been problems in recovery for me and other African Americans.

A whole chapter is dedicated to helping clinicians work more effectively, specifically with African Americans but also with any minority population. This book will assist both the counselor and the African-American client to have a more productive recovery experience. If this book saves one black person from relapsing it will be a success. If one clinician reads it and delivers better quality treatment as a result, it will be a success. If this book serves as a model to individualize a relapse prevention treatment for any other minority group, it will be a success. I have much passion about this topic and I hope this book demonstrates that.

I will use the model of Relapse Prevention Therapy designed by Terence T. Gorski as the foundation of this work. I believe this is currently the most effective model available and has a proven history of success. This model has been used for years throughout the country in treatment centers and individual counseling practices. Thousands of therapists have been trained in this model and hundreds have been certified as Relapse Prevention Specialists. Terry Gorski has continued to modify his work so that it addresses current issues such as brief therapy and managed care. He has revised the training sessions to make them more available, affordable, and effective.

Clinicians and clients using this book should become familiar with Gorski's CENAPS Model of Relapse Prevention Therapy. I recommend *Staying Sober: A Guide to Relapse Prevention* by Terence T. Gorski and Merlene Miller and *The Revised and Simplified Staying Sober Workbook* by Terence T. Gorski. There have been some subsequent publications of the workbook and any edition will do. Take the opportunity to attend a CENAPS-sponsored workshop or Relapse Prevention Certification School to become more familiar with the latest modifications to the model. It was by attending one of these trainings myself that I became dedicated to writing this book.

Terence T. Gorski is listed as coauthor of this book. The reason is simple. Much of the work that he has spent years developing and improving is the basis for this book. I am using models and techniques that he pioneered. I often refer to his published works because this book was designed to work with them. In addition to his past contributions, he has generously provided me with invaluable insight and direction in assisting me in the creation and completion of this book. Without him this book might never have been written. At least not by me.

Chapter 1

Origins of the Model

It was 1986 when I first got into the field of substance-abuse counseling. From the beginning I was interested in relapse prevention. I saw many addicts and alcoholics relapse, and I knew there was much work to be done with this population. In some cases I could see relapse warning signs occur before the actual chemical use, but in other cases the cause of relapse was not so obvious. I often found it hard to predict who would recover. Many of the ones who relapsed I thought would stay clean and many of the ones who stayed clean I thought would relapse. I wanted to learn more about relapse prevention so I could work with those clients who appeared to have given up on recovery. In an attempt to uncover any trends or patterns I decided to keep an eye on the clients I recognized as relapse prone.

One of the first things I noticed was that a large and disproportionate number of blacks were relapsing. In treatment centers and 12-Step meetings blacks often were absent or the extreme minority. I talked with blacks who complained of feeling unwelcome in 12-Step programs and not having anyone to relate to in the treatment centers. Many blacks couldn't afford the hospital programs; the county programs often were filled or had a long waiting list. Many blacks had to return to their neighborhoods or families following treatment, and almost always that meant a "slippery situation." I saw many blacks who had become addicted to the lifestyle: the whole idea of hustling and the fast life characteristic of the drug subculture. I began to think the already slim odds for recovery were even slimmer for blacks. It seemed that once again the deck was stacked against us. At that point I decided to focus on African Americans in recovery. This is where I wanted to make a difference. So I knew I needed to learn as much as I could about relapse prevention.

In the summer of 1987 I first became aware of Terry Gorski's work. I went to a training session that one of his students presented in Redwood City, California. I was fascinated: here was the first clear explanation of relapse as a *process*. His model was easy to understand and highlighted not only the identification but the management of relapse warning signs. I got copies of his videos and audiotapes and studied his work. I began to apply it with my clients in 1988 and was happy to find that it worked. I went to the Relapse Prevention Certification School in 1992, and in 1993 I joined the CENAPS faculty. I was excited to see positive results with my clients of all races. But I noticed that my black clients often would identify warning signs not included in Terry's list. I wondered if we could make this more culturally specific without compromising the integrity of the model.

In January 1996 we held a Relapse Prevention Certification School in Santa Cruz, California. The issue was raised by some of the black students that the model needs to be more "sensitive" to different cultures, specifically African Americans. Terry and I met with several African-American students to share ideas. We discussed differences and similarities between the cultures and agreed there were enough differences within the African-American culture to warrant a specific relapse prevention model. We set up several goals for the project: (1) identify specific warning signs for African Americans; (2) make more recovery options available to black clients and the clinicians working with them; and (3) make a difference in the black community by reducing the number of blacks who relapse. This appeared to be an opportunity to help my community and learn more about relapse prevention. And so, I committed to do some research and write a pamphlet.

Right after the training I formed an advisory committee: a group of black chemical dependency counselors all trained in cultural diversity and relapse prevention. We scheduled meetings to discuss the issues of relapse among African-American addicts and alcoholics. Many hours of lively and emotional conversation produced much excitement and dedication regarding this work. It was apparent to us that this was much needed in the black community and the field of substance-abuse treatment.

I prepared a questionnaire that would ask blacks in treatment about their views and experiences with recovery and race. This informed survey was distributed to several treatment facilities. We began to see first hand what the perceptions were of our own needs as a people regarding race and recovery. From the two hundred responses I identified high-risk thoughts, feelings, and action urges. The results affirmed what we already suspected. For the black clients who relapsed, race was often a contributing factor. As a matter of fact, race was a constant issue for blacks in recovery, seeking acceptance into support groups, and gaining access to treatment. Self-image and hopes for the future were frequently impacted by the individual's perceptions of race. So I began to write.

I wrote the twenty-two Relapse Warning Signs for African Americans and the Guidelines for the Clinician. I tried to explain the results of the survey, along with my experience as a clinician and a black man. This book was written, with passion and hope, for all those black folks affected by the disease of addiction and all those working with them.

In the book I use the terms "African American" and "black" interchangeably. I do so for both convenience and to honor those who might prefer either term. When I refer to addiction I mean to drugs and/or alcohol. When I refer to a specific gender it does not represent any kind of sexism; it could be male or female in most cases.

Chapter 2

Addiction and the
Black Community

At the core of all addiction is an internal belief that says to the addict, "I'm not OK," "I'm somehow inadequate," and "I must drink, smoke, snort, shoot, buy, wear, screw, or eat something to be better." All addicts and alcoholics struggle with feeling less than, different, and excluded. In most treatment facilities, listing low self-esteem as a treatment problem is no longer tolerated. It's taken for granted that the addict and alcoholic will have issues related to low self-esteem. Other generic issues usually present with addicts and alcoholics include: denial, rationalization, distrust, manipulation, isolation, resentment, and blaming. These are good examples of simple recovery issues that are common to all substance abusers. However, when you are working with African Americans these issues have an added dimension.

Think about alcoholism and drug addiction. Consider the severe spiritual, biological, psychological, and social wreckage that's created for the addicted individual. Think of how the addict's self-image and perception of the future is impacted. Think of his sense of isolation and opinion of how others might view him. Think of his fear and sense of helplessness. Now consider the African American's situation.

Many blacks have all the above characteristics *before* the onset of the addiction. Quite a few blacks live their whole life struggling and feeling second class even without drugs and alcohol. Furthermore, we live in a society that has perpetuated many negative images about how blacks think and live. Drugs and alcohol don't create a monster within the average black addict; they just feed the monster that is already there. And the monster didn't just arrive; it was bred and nurtured.

Hundreds of years of discrimination have had an impact on black culture. You cannot subject a group of people to decades or racism, torture, exclusion, and abuse without seeing severe repercussion. It wasn't that long ago when blacks couldn't vote, eat in the same restaurants, or drink from the same water fountains as whites. This type of treatment was commonplace and accepted by many. As a result, various coping strategies were passed on from one generation of blacks to the next. What do you think was their legacy? What do you think they learned about themselves and others? What do you think the older blacks taught the youngsters?

The legacy was sad. Many blacks came to believe they were second-class citizens who shouldn't expect to be treated as equals. Subsequently, feelings of inadequacy, distrustful views about other races and negative views of themselves have crippled the black community for years. Racism has had a deep-rooted impact on black culture, and we are continuing to identify and repair its damage. When drugs and alcohol were introduced to black culture the effects were devastating. When you have an already handicapped culture and add addiction to the mix, the bad gets worse. A good example of this is my own visits to my childhood home.

When I go back to my old neighborhood on the south side of Chicago, it literally brings tears to my eyes. Sixty-third

Street, which was once a vibrant Mecca of cultural excitement, is now a barren wasteland. It looks like a war zone. Drugs have destroyed the community and the families I knew as a child. It's like a type of genocide is taking place right before our eyes. It saddens me even more when I realize that people capitalize on this tragedy.

Almost unique in the black community is the fact that drugs often bring money into the household. The teenage drug dealer buys homes, cars, and jewelry for his family off the profits from the poison he sells to his own people. It's very difficult to persuade a young hustler that a job in a fast food restaurant is better than selling drugs. The music industry has catered to the market and glamorizes this destructive lifestyle. Liquor stores on every corner sell brands of fortified wines and malt liquors usually only seen in minority communities. Strategically placed, "culturally sensitive" billboards are glaring with promises of sexiness, wealth, and success if you drink or smoke their brand. The chaos and tension present in many black neighborhoods would be intolerable to many of those who have never experienced it.

The murders, mayhem, and madness committed in our communities are unparalleled in this country. Take one look at the country's penal system and see the one place where we clearly are the majority. Drugs and alcohol are killing black society through AIDS, incarceration, and the slavery of addiction. If something doesn't change, the future looks bleak.

I heard Maya Angelou, a beautiful black poet, once say that she had "shed tears for our great-grandparents who worked so hard that one day we might have a better life. They would turn over in their graves to see what has become of us now." Something needs to be done. Black addicts and alcoholics must know that recovery is possible. We need a concentrated effort to reach out to this population before it's too late. There is no reason to allow this tragedy to continue. Culturally specific models of treatment and relapse prevention are a necessary move in the right direction.

Chapter 3

Statistics

With the help of my advisory committee and other counselors working in various treatment settings, I surveyed more than 250 African Americans in recovery and received approximately 200 completed surveys. These are the results. I want to reiterate that this is a nonscientific, informal survey that was done simply to begin to examine blacks' perceptions of race as a factor in their recovery. It is important to consider that this survey was given to black addicts and alcoholics during a course of treatment. I chose not to survey blacks who had relapsed and were still using drugs or alcohol. I wanted the reporting to be as clear and thoughtful as possible. Nevertheless, the results are revealing and thought provoking. (A copy of the survey is located at the end of this chapter.)

45 percent cited race as a factor in relapse
Of those surveyed 45 percent had relapsed, and this was at least their second attempt at recovery. That's not surprising, however. Remember that many of those relapsers were still using and therefore unable to participate in this survey. I suspect, without proof, that blacks have a higher relapse rate than other addicts and alcoholics. What's most signifi-

cant about this section is the fact that of those who relapse, 45 percent believe race was a factor. I would not expect that white relapsers would attribute race as a factor in their relapse. This implies that the participants in this survey believe their race adds another dimension to their recovery, which contributes to relapse.

48 percent feel they have more relapse triggers

Of those surveyed 48 percent reported they have more relapse triggers because they are black. They reported that being black adds additional hardships to the already difficult task of recovery. Many of the additional triggers were related to racism: perceived lack of employment opportunities, unsafe living situations, lack of appropriate support systems, and feeling different or excluded. Of those surveyed 35 percent stated that being black actually hurt their chances for recovery. They believe that nonblacks have more and better opportunities for recovery.

39 percent experience a "lot of racism" in recovery

Of those surveyed 39 percent stated they had experienced a "lot of racism" in recovery. I deliberately asked participants to report excessive racism. It is disturbing to consider that in a so-called recovery atmosphere there is a perception of extreme racism. Participants in the survey disclosed situations where they were referred to as "niggers" or other racial slurs; omitted from social functions because of their race; or denied sponsorship, hugs, phone numbers, etc. because of racism. In treatment settings, group therapy was felt to be threatening and unsafe as nonblacks shared their resentment about blacks. Many felt that white counselors treated them unfairly because of racism. Although it is important to report these findings, we must remember that perceptions are not facts.

Many blacks may perceive that racism is present when,

in fact, it might not be. Oftentimes racism is considered to be the underlying cause of negative actions directed at blacks, even when it's not. But in this case I am more concerned with the fact that blacks believe racism is abundant, rather than the actual reasons surrounding the incident. In other words, real or imagined, if one perceives he is being victimized by racism then his actions will reflect that. Therefore, we must consider this issue valid.

28 percent do not feel welcome in 12-Step meetings

There were two primary complaints about 12-Step meetings. Many of those surveyed felt there weren't enough other blacks in the meetings. They stated that everyone appeared cliquish and they were treated as outcasts or intruders. They also complained that the 12-Step philosophy was forced on them and conflicted with their spiritual beliefs. Some didn't like the idea of "God as you understand Him," and they felt that wasn't specific enough. Others didn't believe in God and rejected the 12-Step programs as cult-like, with a religious agenda.

37 percent do not feel they have enough black role models

Many blacks don't feel there are enough positive black role models in general. Often young blacks see sports and music stars as examples of achievable success. In the inner cities it is often the drug dealers or other criminals with the money and flashy cars that attract the young minds. Many of the blacks taking the survey complained that they don't see enough clean and sober blacks actively working programs of recovery. They reported difficulty finding appropriate black sponsors, and in treatment settings they saw few black counselors. They experienced frustration when seeking professional referrals to black licensed therapists.

Relapse Prevention for African Americans: Informal Survey

Part One

Name: _____ Age: _____ Sex: ____

Drug/s of choice: _____ Number of years using: _____

How long have you been clean and sober? _____

Please answer the following questions based on your own personal experience in recovery. (Circle one answer.)

1. Have you relapsed since you've been clean and sober? **yes** **no**

2. If you did relapse, do you think it had anything to do with being black? **yes** **no**

3. Do you think you have more relapse triggers because you're black? **yes** **no**

4. Do you experience a lot of racism in recovery? **yes** **no**

5. As a black person do you feel welcome in 12-Step groups? **yes** **no**

6. Do you have enough black role models who are clean and sober? **yes** **no**

7. Do you think being black has helped you in recovery or hurt you in recovery? **helped** **hurt**

Part Two

Please complete the following sentences with a different answer:

I know my recovery is in trouble when I think: _____

_____

_____

I know my recovery is in trouble when I think: _____

_____

_____

I know my recovery is in trouble when I think: _____

_____

_____

I know my recovery is in trouble when I feel: _____

_____

_____

I know my recovery is in trouble when I feel: _____

_____

_____

I know my recovery is in trouble when I feel: _____

_____

_____

I know my recovery is in trouble when I have an urge to:

_____

_____

I know my recovery is in trouble when I have an urge to:

_____

_____

I know my recovery is in trouble when I have an urge to:

_____

_____

I know my recovery is in trouble when what I actually do

is: _____

_____

I know my recovery is in trouble when what I actually do

is: _____

_____

I know my recovery is in trouble when what I actually do

is: _____

_____

Chapter 4

High-Risk Thoughts, Feelings, and Action Urges

To identify high-risk TFAU's I asked participants in the survey to report what thoughts, feelings, and action urges indicate that their recovery is in trouble. I am listing the top five responses most frequently listed by the survey participants. Each section shows paraphrases of the response and the number of times that response was given. Each participant was asked to respond three times to each section. I came to some conclusions as I interpreted this information. Those conclusions follow each section.

High-Risk Thoughts	
1. "I'm cured" or "I'm above the rules"	90
2. "I can use" or "I want to use"	87
3. "I'm not OK" or "I'm inadequate"	53
4. "It won't work for me"	28
5. "There's a conspiracy to keep me down"	28

In looking at the high-risk thoughts, I was surprised to find that the number-one thought was feeling cured or above the rules. Thoughts that suggested immunity and entitlement as well as a disregard for basic recovery principles dominated. These were followed closely by thoughts of using drugs or alcohol, usually thoughts of substituting rather than using the drug of choice. The next three thoughts dealt with low self-esteem and victimization: those taking the survey reported thoughts about a conspiracy to keep them down and an idea that recovery won't work for them so why bother. It's not surprising that many blacks have difficulty following the rules when there is some perception that the rules were not made with their best interests in mind. In some more extreme cases the perception is that the rules were made specifically to oppress blacks.

High-Risk Feelings	
1. Depression	97
2. Different/Excluded	79
3. Loneliness	61
4. Anger	53
5. Inadequacy	28

The number-one high-risk feeling was related to depression. Feelings of hopelessness, helplessness, sadness, and despair topped the list. Second was feeling different and excluded. Third was loneliness, followed by anger. Look at the process: addicts get depressed (and few blacks seek treatment for depression—it's almost considered par for the course) and because they feel different and excluded they perceive that they have fewer resources; then they get lonely and finally angry. The next feeling, inadequacy, shows up after the anger and may relate to the inability to handle the preceding emotions.

High-Risk Action Urges	
1. To go back to the old lifestyle, fast money, slippery places, etc.	98
2. To use drugs or alcohol	75
3. To isolate or shut down, avoid people in recovery	37
4. To use sex to fix, gain power, or self-worth	33
5. To give up on recovery	33

The high-risk action urges are no surprise; the number-one urge is to go back to the old lifestyle. Consider that black addicts are thinking about using and thinking that they may be cured; follow that with feeling depressed, excluded, and lonely in recovery, and it makes sense that the urge would be to go someplace where they feel a connection. Going back to old playgrounds, playmates, and playthings was the most common response. Participants in the survey frequently described getting involved in old behaviors that support the addictive lifestyle. These behaviors appeared to give the client some sense of familiarity.

The second high-risk urge was to use drugs or alcohol, and again, substituting another drug for the drug of choice came up. Next was the urge to shut down or isolate, avoid discussing recovery issues, and stop associating with recovering people. The next urge was to fix with sex, usually high-risk sex with partners and in situations that would threaten their recovery. Many participants stated they would use sex to feel better, even though they might jeopardize their recovery in the process. Sex with prostitutes or former using partners were frequent choices. Finally was the thought to give up on recovery altogether ("Why bother? It's not working for me and I feel miserable").

This data clearly demonstrates that blacks have many issues related to their culture. These issues can either enhance or impair their recovery process. Most often these issues go completely unaddressed or are inappropriately discussed in treatment settings, and many black clients relapse as a result. This book provides for the first time twenty-two Relapse Warning Signs for African Americans* that address culturally specific issues that contribute to the relapse process. Black clients will be provided a tool that will help them to identify and manage these warning signs and hopefully avoid relapse.

---

* *Relapse Warning Signs for African Americans: A Culturally Specific Model* is available in booklet form from Herald House/Independence Press (1997); 1-800-767-8181.

Chapter 5

Guidelines for Clinicians: Working with Chemically Dependent African Americans

This section is designed primarily to assist counselors and therapists to be more effective, confident, and competent in working with African Americans. Even though the issues discussed are specific to African Americans, they are certainly not limited to African Americans. The following suggestions are useful to consider whenever you are working with a minority or culturally diverse group or individual. These guidelines are generic enough to be applied in any cross-cultural counseling situation. I would strongly suggest that close attention be paid to this section, because many mistakes in treatment occur because of inadequate consideration of these topics.

1. Self-Assessment: Identifying Your Prejudices and Limitations

Before you can assess any client it is important that you examine and identify your own preconceived ideas about this particular group or individual. What has been your experience with this population? Have your experiences and / or views tainted your interaction style? It is important to identify your own prejudices, primarily because it makes it clearer when you are attempting to work with your client's issues. Oftentimes the counselor's issues get confused as the client's issues. The old saying, "If you can't name it, you can't tame it," comes to mind. Many people would rather think of themselves as "prejudice free" or think they've "worked through" those issues. It somehow means something negative to admit that you are, in fact, the not-so-proud possessor of racist attitudes or beliefs.

In reality, we all have racism to certain degrees. So become aware of what feelings and attitudes *really* exist for you regarding African Americans and don't allow yourself to be blind-sided during a therapy session. Certainly it's a form of countertransference that can be owned and managed.

Some issues to consider might be: How do you feel when a big black man walks into your office? What do you think of the slang that many blacks tend to use? the "chip on the shoulder" attitude? the fondness for gold jewelry and flashy clothes? the stereotypes of blacks as criminals and lazy manipulators of the system? Maybe some blacks have been aggressive and rude to you, blaming society for their problems. Maybe you are somehow embarrassed or ashamed because of the oppression blacks have endured in this country. Are you willing to confront a black person the same way you would someone of your own race? Do you find yourself talking differently to blacks than you would to someone of your own race? Do you use the "N-word"? How do you feel about blacks using the N-word? Would you want a black to marry your sister, brother, or child? If not, why not?

These questions are designed to help identify your own issues that may be unresolved and even unrealized. Discussing and deciding what prejudices you actually own is the beginning of more effective cross-cultural counseling. You put yourself in a much better position to understand the difference between your agenda and the client's. You may also decide that your issues prevent you from being fair and effective and therefore choose to have someone else work with these clients. That's appropriate at times. The primary concern here is that clients get the best possible care, which is exactly what they deserve.

I might add that racism does not always manifest itself in negative and abusive words and actions. Many blacks receive extra-favorable treatment from nonblacks who want to somehow express their solidarity and support for the black cause, whatever that is. Special treatment is not in the best interest of the individual and often is counterproductive in terms of their personal growth. In any event, treating someone differently based solely on the color of their skin is racism. If you are treating someone differently because you've determined that it's necessary to address their specific individual clinical needs, that's certainly not the same as treating them differently because it somehow makes you feel better. Examine your motivation whenever you feel a client is getting preferential treatment from you.

2. Stereotyping and Overgeneralization

Just as all addicts aren't the same, not all blacks are the same. It's difficult to be sensitive to black issues when they often appear totally different depending on which black person you're talking to. I remember being in organizations where a black client would walk in, and automatically he would be referred to me. The idea was that we would be able to work better together because we were both black—when in reality, there have been cases where the *only* thing we had in common was our race. The black cultural experience is in itself so diverse that one can easily do more harm than good in trying to address the cultural needs of black clients.

Blacks often have completely different views and identity issues depending on what part of the country they're from, what level of education, what part of the neighborhood, what complexion, and what kind of family they were raised in. A good example would be the terminology used to refer to black Americans. I remember when we were called Negroes and "Colored folks"; at that time it was an insult to call someone black. Then during the 1960s black "got beautiful" and it became an insult to call someone "Colored" or Negro. Then came African American, a term that certainly has become more popular in the nineties. But don't assume that the latest term is necessarily the best one to use. I suggest that rather than say the wrong thing and have it be the focus of your session time, ask the client privately what he prefers to be called.

Beware of generalizations and stereotyping. The best advice is to use good therapeutic skills. Develop a treatment plan that takes into account your client's unique and specific clinical needs. In some cases the client's race will be more of an issue than in others. Not every black person will have barriers that are created and nurtured by their ethnicity. With other clients it will dominate the focus of your treatment.

3. Adaptation and Coping Styles

A variation of the following model was made popular by Peter Bell and Jimmy Evans in their book *Counseling the Black Client: Alcohol Use and Abuse in Black America* (Hazelden, 1981). It may be a helpful tool to determine treatment approaches for your black clients. It addresses how individuals adapt to the dominant culture and where they feel most comfortable. In viewing this model it's apparent that the same approach will not work for every black client. I will look at three client types and show that the clinical needs for each client may be totally different. The client types listed below are not meant to be absolutes, merely brief examples of different coping styles.

Client A: Centered in Black Culture

- Has made no attempt to fit into the majority culture.
- May be described by some as a separatist and maybe even a racist.
- Might wear African garb and associate primarily with other blacks.
- Has little interest or desire to be accepted and approved of by the dominant culture.
- May often see nonblacks as the enemy or someone who doesn't understand his issues.
- Feels much more comfortable with other blacks and avoids nonblacks.
- Distrusts and has difficulty relating with nonblacks.

This client type can be the most difficult for nonblack counselors to work with, and he might be even more difficult for a black counselor who is centered in white culture (see the next client type). In dealing with this client, you might often see anger, resistance, and denial. He might excuse or explain his behavior by describing it as retaliation for racial oppression against blacks. He might demonstrate a sense of entitlement that causes power struggles, and be very distrustful of the counselor and his or her techniques. He might be resistant to taking responsibility for his addiction, instead blaming it on racism. He can be controlling and antagonistic, and will most likely trigger any unresolved racial issues for the counselor.

Client B: Centered in White Culture

- Does everything possible to fit in and be accepted by the white middle-class dominant culture.

- May be described by some as an "Uncle Tom" or "house Negro."
- Tries hard to gain the approval of nonblack friends.
- Avoids contact with other blacks and has little connection to the black community.
- Often sees other blacks as the enemy and/or a source of shame and embarrassment.
- Has difficulty trusting other blacks and usually feels "better than" or "less than."
- Often will adapt speech and mannerisms that mimic the dominant culture.
- May not like being reminded of being black.

This client type will prefer to work with a white counselor, and will get uncomfortable around other blacks. He will resist having his race be a topic of conversation and may feel superior to other blacks and demonstrate strong racist views against his own race. He is usually articulate and well educated with a sophisticated denial and rationalization system.

Client C: Bicultural

- Is able to function well in both cultures.
- Might sometimes feel bilingual or socially schizophrenic.
- Can speak the language of the dominant culture then go into the black community and switch to another language and mannerism.
- Feels a connection and loyalty to both worlds.
- Does not feel that being black requires exclusivity.
- Periodically feels pressure from both worlds to conform.
- Because of the ability to be in both cultures, will demonstrate the best and worst of each.
- Is often privy to conversations the separatist doesn't hear.
- Is most likely to use a larger support system in recovery due to the exposure and comfort experienced in both cultures.

For this client, race will not be a primary focus of treatment. However, there is a possibility of feeling disconnected in both the white and black worlds. He might describe feeling like he's in limbo between the two cultures. His ability to move from one culture to the next can be used as escapism in certain situations. For example, when hurt or pressured by his white friends, he can retreat to the black community or black "mannerisms" for comfort and vice versa. This can be confusing and painful to the client and his friends. This client will expect to be treated as an individual and will resist stereotyping.

4. Counseling vs. Education

As tempting as it might be, don't use your counseling session as an opportunity to learn more about black culture. Therapists often find themselves fascinated as their black clients give them first-hand knowledge of the inner workings of black culture. Finding out what makes a black person tick may be much more interesting than the assignment that's due. The time spent with the client is *his* time; if *you're* benefiting more than he is, something is wrong. This isn't to say that wanting to learn more about black culture from blacks isn't a good idea; just don't use your clients as teachers or your counseling sessions as a classroom. Take classes and workshops, read books written by blacks, and spend time with your black friends. If you don't have any black friends, go back to number one in this section.

Sometimes the client may also feel it's his duty to teach you how black people think and feel. That is not the purpose of the session, and the client should be made aware of that. Again, the primary focus is the client and whether he is getting what he needs to achieve and maintain recovery.

5. How It Relates to the Addiction

This is a tricky one. As you know, addicts often like to talk about anything other than what they need to do to recover. Many will find a million ways to divert the focus from the primary issue of addiction. Often they are looking for ways to avoid confrontation and feedback. Well, the race issue is a perfect distraction. You may find a black client wanting to talk about racial topics rather than the steps or the assignment you gave him for homework. You may notice that every time you touch on a hot issue he changes the subject to a racial topic. Now here is the tricky part.

When you refuse to talk about the black stuff and instead insist on talking about the recovery stuff you might be labeled as insensitive and discounting. While honoring the cultural diversity of your client you must remember what your primary purpose is. Your number-one agenda is to help the client get and stay clean and sober.

Any issue the client raises may be important. However, the questions you must ask are: "How does this relate to the addiction?" "How has this contributed to your using?" and "How is it going to prevent you from staying clean and sober?"

Especially in the days of task-oriented, brief therapy and managed care, we don't have the luxury of wasting sessions on issues that don't relate directly to recovery. So gently remind the client that although you are interested in his views and opinions regarding race, you would be short-changing him if you didn't bring the discussion back to the task at hand: how to get and stay clean and sober.

6. Don't Minimize Your Own Qualifications

Take a moment to rate your own clinical skills as a therapist. A ten means you believe you provide top-quality counseling in a compassionate and professional manner. A one indicates you need another job. I'll bet you feel pretty good overall about the work you do. And why shouldn't you? Can you work effectively with clients who feel depressed, have denial, or don't trust you? Can you do conflict resolution and active listening? Are you familiar with chemical dependency and relapse prevention? Do you know how and when to confront a client? Can you read nonverbal communication? Can you facilitate a group? Can you do a lecture? Well, it sounds like you know your stuff.

Don't minimize your own capabilities because you might be working with a different culture. Don't back down when you get accused of not knowing what you're talking about. Don't allow your own fears, insecurities, and self-doubt to cause you to abandon all your training. You don't have to have walked in someone's shoes to be able to help them. You don't have to know all the inner workings of each culture in order to be effective. The most important description of a good therapist is: "Know what you're talking about and care about your client." If you can communicate that to your clients, you're in great shape. Remember: use your skills.

7. Individualize Treatment Based on Specific Clinical Needs

If you are reading this you must have an interest in cross-cultural counseling. You want to be more effective working with blacks and hopefully other minorities. You want to know as much as you can about the different cultures so you can provide better treatment. Well, by now you must have figured out that black culture is pretty complicated and diverse. How can you possibly study and learn enough to be prepared for the "type" of black client that might show up in your office? And it's not just black clients who are complicated.

What about the Hispanic client? Is he Cuban, Puerto Rican, Mexican? first or second generation? What about the Native American client? Which tribe is he from? What part of the country? How about Asians or Pacific Islanders? And culture isn't just race related. How much do you know about gay and lesbian issues? How about the different drugs people use? Do you know about the culture of people who smoke PCP versus people who smoke crack? Do you know about those who use "Ecstasy" and go to "Raves"? Do you understand the difference between people who shoot heroin and those who smoke it? That's all a bit overwhelming, isn't it? Well it certainly is. There is no way for any therapist to be knowledgable about every culture that he might wind up working with. So what's the answer?

Individualized treatment is the key. If you treat each of your clients as an individual with specific individual clinical needs, your treatment will be a success. You don't need to be pregnant to work with a pregnant woman, and you don't need to be black to work with a black client. However, you do need to avoid generalizing and stereotyping. If you do a thorough assessment and identify clinical issues that might influence treatment, you can be effective. You will see common issues that all addicts and alcoholics deal with, but they might be communicated or influenced differently based on cultural experience. If you do a truly individualized treatment plan, you will always be in a better position to provide quality, professional, and competent care.

Chapter 6

Working with Clients: Problems and Concerns

The following issues should be discussed as potential problems the clinician may encounter while attempting to work with black clients. All addicts and alcoholics have similar relapse issues; however, black clients have an additional set of issues specific to their culture. Therefore, black clients who use the twenty-two Relapse Warning Signs for African Americans should also be asked to review the Relapse Warning Signs List developed by Terence T. Gorski. This list will demonstrate the relapse process and prepare clients to better understand the concept of warning signs. However, this obviously involves more work for the client. It's important to prepare your clients in advance that this work is task driven and will require much time and effort on their part, but point out that the rewards justify the effort.

You may discover that every black client will not have race as a primary issue in their recovery. If it's not an issue, don't make it one. I strongly suggest you become familiar with the Relapse Warning Signs for African Americans, and if you see a client who appears to be experiencing one of the warning signs, offer him or her the list.

You may have problems if you work in a multicultural setting and you give the black client a set of separate warning signs. What impact might that have on the other clients? What about the black client? Will it contribute to focusing more on the differences rather than the similarities? Will it encourage the clients to get closer together or further apart? How do you maintain that delicate blend of commonality and individualism?

The goal here is not to build more stumbling blocks in the recovery path of the black client. On the contrary it is to implement a tool that will allow the client to see obstacles more clearly. The black client is being taught to honor and verbalize issues that may, in fact, cost him his recovery if they go unnoticed. So it is critical that the black client understand that in discussing these warning signs you are not suggesting that he use them in any way to limit his recovery but instead use them as a vehicle to enhance his recovery.

As for the nonblack clients, who will not have an individualized and specific warning sign list, CENAPS is currently working to produce other relapse warning sign lists that address sexuality and occupational issues as well as other cultures. In the meantime, I recommend that you work with your clients to identify specific relapse warning signs that they feel are related to their particular culture. This can be an enlightening and empowering process for the client and the therapist. The twenty-two Relapse Warning Signs for African Americans can be used as an example if needed.

I hope that clinicians will not be discouraged by the potential problems that may result in utilizing this tool. Issues may arise that cause conflict and confusion for the clients and the clinician, but it is a tremendous opportunity for growth and healing. If it is used correctly, the client will be able to overcome issues that may otherwise result in relapse.

Chapter 7

The Relapse Process

"Relapse is part of recovery." I have heard that said many times, and I know that many addicts and alcoholics interpret that to mean that they'll relapse. They often have misconceptions about relapse, so they think this means they will drink or use again. Although the saying is true, it requires a bit of an explanation.

First, it needs to be noted that you can relapse without using drugs or alcohol. We know that relapse is a process, not an event, and it occurs long before the addict actually uses drugs. Second, in order to relapse you have to be in recovery. If you're not in recovery you are not relapsing—you are using. So clear definitions of recovery must be established. Refer to chapter four in *Staying Sober: A Guide to Relapse Prevention* by Terence T. Gorski and Merlene Miller for a good definition of recovery. Third, the saying almost gives addicts permission to use again: because it's "part of recovery," why fight it? But the reality is many addict/alcoholics never drink or use after their first attempt at recovery. Actually, almost a third remain totally abstinent from the beginning.

I also hear many people refer to relapses as "slips," which to me implies that the addict was walking down the street and accidentally "slipped" and wound up with a bottle in her mouth or a syringe in her arm. I think the term "slip" minimizes the relapse and discourages the addict from really identifying the warning signs that preceded the relapse. Somewhere I read that "slip" stands for "Sobriety Losing Its Priority." It's important that addicts thoroughly examine each relapse episode and each period of recovery in order to identify warning signs, self-defeating patterns, and strengths and weaknesses. To minimize or ignore a relapse is a setup for future relapses.

We know that abstinence is not recovery. Abstinence is a prerequisite for recovery. The addict must be abstinent in order to be clear enough to do the work that needs to be done in recovery. Recovery is a process that involves biopsychosocial healing. That work is often difficult and emotional; without abstinence the addict doesn't have a chance.

There are many cases where addicts with several years of not drinking or using wind up fighting, stealing, selling drugs, getting arrested, sexualizing, and/or committing suicide. They get into what's commonly called a "dry drunk"; this is part of the relapse process and clearly illustrates that even without drinking and using one can be in full-blown relapse. Old behaviors and thinking patterns ("stinking thinking") can resurface, and the addict can feel completely out of touch with recovery even though he may not have cravings to use.

So recovery is much more than not drinking or using. It's a commitment to a different lifestyle, one that involves growth and change. Scott Peck describes love in his book *The Road Less Traveled* as, "The will to extend oneself for the purpose of nurturing one's own or another's spiritual growth." I think that is a good definition for recovery as well.

Chapter 8

Using the Relapse Warning Signs List

Why do we need a separate set of warning signs for African Americans? When discussing relapse among African Americans it is important to identify a few issues that arise. What is the extent of the problem for blacks in recovery? How much of a role does race play in relapse and recovery? Again, I want to refer to the data in my survey of two hundred black addicts and alcoholics in which 45 percent of them had relapsed. And 45 percent of those who relapsed felt that being black contributed to their relapse. Almost half of them believed they had more relapse triggers because of their race. A full 39 percent felt they experience a *lot* of racism in recovery, and 28 percent don't feel welcome in 12-Step meetings. Sadly 37 percent don't feel they have enough black role models in recovery, and most disturbing is the fact that 35 percent believe being black hurts their recovery process.

This certainly suggests there is a need for a culturally specific plan of action that addresses these issues. The fact that recovery is not perceived as inviting to some simply because of race is a problem. If black addicts and alcoholics don't feel welcome, accepted, or understood in recovery, then there's a good chance we will see a higher number of relapses.

There are relapse warning signs that all addicts and alcoholics may experience. These will be demonstrated in the next chapter with the Relapse Warning Signs List and the Brief Warning Signs List developed by Terence T. Gorski. In addition to these, we have a unique set of warning signs that address issues specific to black culture. So even though we acknowledge that on some level all addicts and alcoholics are the same, we also want to accept the differences. We want to discourage "terminal uniqueness" but at the same time allow blacks to discuss and process cultural issues that may threaten their recovery. We want to truly individualize the treatment process for all of our clients and use this tool to assist the black clients in particular to address their specific clinical needs.

I am convinced that blacks have many particular circumstances, ideas, and views. The purpose of the Relapse Warning Signs for African Americans is to identify and honor that diversity. Even though the underlying issues in these twenty-two warning signs are not exclusive to blacks, the perception and experience of each issue is our own and therefore unique.

I have found the Relapse Warning Signs for African Americans to be an effective tool to prompt group and individual discussion. Blacks and nonblacks have demonstrated much interest in the topics raised by these warning signs. In most cases, I was unable to complete the list because the discussion generated was so intense. I am confident that all addicts and alcoholics can relate to many of the underlying recovery issues contained in each warning sign.

I suggest that clinicians experiment with the material. Use what you can, when you can. Be willing to take risks and allow your clients to do likewise. The experience can be rewarding for both the client and the clinician.

The CENAPS warning sign lists in the following chapters can be used in a number of ways. For the purpose of client education they can be read as a group exercise or in an individual session. Clients can be asked to identify issues that seem to pertain to them. The relapse-prone client will need more focused relapse prevention therapy. In such cases it is suggested that the warning signs be used according to directions as they appear in the CENAPS workbooks.

Chapter 9

The Original CENAPS Relapse Warning Signs List

The following pages contain a copy of the original CENAPS Warning Signs List written by Terence T. Gorski. This list demonstrates the phases and warning signs of relapse. It is probably the most popular and often-used list of relapse triggers. Many relapse-prone addicts and alcoholics have found hope after reviewing this list. It helped them to believe there was a solution. The relapse process became much less confusing. This was one of the first published accounts of the relapse process. It gave a clear and easy-to-understand description of the progression from stable recovery to relapse. In my clinical experience it continues to be a most effective tool for guiding clients in identifying their own relapse warning signs.

Phase 1:   Internal Change

I start to notice that something is going wrong. I'm still working a recovery program and look good on the outside, but I'm using old ways of thinking and managing feelings that make me feel bad on the inside. I'm concerned, but I don't know what's wrong or what to do about it. The most common relapse warning signs are:

☐ 1-1   *Increased Stress:* I begin to feel more stressed than usual. Sometimes this is the result of a problem or situation that's easy to see. At other times it's the result of little problems that cause stress to build up slowly over time.

☐ 1-2   *Change in Thinking:* I begin to think that my recovery program isn't as important as it used to be. Sometimes things are going so well that I don't believe I need to put a lot of effort into my program. At other times I have problems that my recovery program doesn't seem to help, and I ask myself "Why bother?"

☐ 1-3   *Change in Feeling:* I start having unpleasant feelings that I don't like. Sometimes I feel euphoric, like everything is going my way when I know that it really isn't. At other times I feel depressed, like nothing is working out. I know that these mood sweeps aren't good for me.

☐ 1-4   *Change in Behavior:* I start acting different. I still look and sound good on the outside, but I know deep inside that I'm not practicing my recovery program the way I used to, and that something is going wrong.

Stop reading and take a moment to identify one of the warning signs that you've just read that stood out to you most.

1. Which warning sign stood out to you?_____

    _____

2. Why did it stand out? _____

    _____

Phase 2: Denial

I stop paying attention to others or honestly telling them what I'm thinking and feeling. I convince myself that everything is OK when it really isn't. The most common relapse warning signs are:

☐ 2-1   ***Worrying about Myself:*** I feel uneasy about the changes in my thinking, feelings, and behavior. This uneasiness comes and goes and usually lasts only a short time. Sometimes I feel afraid that I won't be able to stay in recovery, but I don't want to think about it.

☐ 2-2   ***Denying that I'm Worried:*** I deal with this uneasiness by using old self-defeating ways of thinking and acting. I start lying to myself about what's happening and try to convince myself that everything is OK when it really isn't. Sometimes I believe the lies I tell myself and I can forget my problems and feel better for a little while. I usually can't tell when

I'm lying to myself until later. It's only when I think or talk about the situation later that I'm able to recognize how bad I was feeling and how I denied those feelings.

Stop reading and take a moment to identify one of the warning signs that you've just read that stood out to you most.

1. Which warning sign stood out to you?_____

_____

2. Why did it stand out? _____

_____

Phase 3:   Avoidance and Defensiveness

I try to avoid anyone or anything that will force me to be honest about how my thinking, feelings, and behavior have changed. If I'm directly confronted, I get defensive and can't hear what others are trying to tell me. The most common relapse warning signs are:

☐ 3-1   *Believing I'll Never Relapse:* I convince myself that I don't need to put a lot of energy into my recovery program because I'll never relapse. I don't tell the people involved in my recovery program about this because I know they'll give me a hard time. I tell myself that it's none of their business.

☐ 3-2   *Focusing on Others Instead of Myself:* I take the focus off of myself by becoming more concerned about the recovery of others than about my own recovery. I privately judge my friends, spouse, and other recovering people. I keep these judgments to myself unless others confront me. Then I try to turn the tables by criticizing them. This is often called working the other guy's program.

☐ 3-3 ***Getting Defensive:*** I don't want to tell others what I'm thinking and doing because I'm afraid they'll criticize or confront me. I feel scared, angry, and defensive when other people ask me questions or point out things about my recovery that I don't want to see. I tend to get defensive even when no defense is necessary.

☐ 3-4 ***Getting Compulsive:*** I start using compulsive behaviors to keep my mind off of how uncomfortable I'm feeling. I get stuck in old, rigid, and self-defeating ways of thinking and acting. I try to control conversations, either by talking too much or by not talking at all. I start working more than I need to and get over-involved in many activities. Other people think I'm the model of recovery because of my heavy involvement in self-help groups. I tend to act like a therapist to others but I'm reluctant to talk about my personal problems. I avoid casual or informal involvement with people unless I can be in control.

☐ 3-5 ***Acting Impulsively:*** I start creating problems for myself by using poor judgment and impulsively doing things without thinking them through. This usually happens in times of high stress. Sometimes I privately feel bad but I tend to make excuses and blame others for my problems.

☐ 3-6 *Getting Lonely:* I start spending more time alone because I feel uncomfortable around others. I usually have good reasons and excuses for staying away from other people. I start feeling lonely. Instead of dealing with the loneliness by trying to meet and be around other people, I get more compulsive about doing things alone.

Stop reading and take a moment to identify one of the warning signs that you've just read that stood out to you most.

1. Which warning sign stood out to you?_____

_____

2. Why did it stand out? _____

_____

Phase 4:   Crisis Building

I start having problems in recovery that I don't understand. Even though I want to solve these problems and I work hard at it, two new problems pop up to replace every problem that I solve. The most common warning signs are:

☐ 4-1 *Seeing Only a Small Part of the Problem:* I start thinking that my life is made up of separate and unrelated parts. I focus on one small part of my life and block out everything else. Sometimes I focus only on the good things and block out or ignore the bad. In this way I can mistakenly believe everything is fine when it really isn't. At other times I see only the things that are going wrong and blow them out of proportion. This causes me to feel like nothing is going my way even when there are many good things happening in my life. I can't see the "big picture" or figure out how the things I do in one part of my life can cause problems in other parts of my life. When problems develop, I don't know why.

☐ 4-2 ***Getting Depressed:*** I believe that life is unfair and that I have no power to do anything about it. I feel depressed, down, blue, listless, and empty of feelings. I lack energy, tend to sleep too much, and rarely feel good or full of life. At times I'm able to distract myself from these moods by getting busy with other things and not talking about the depression.

☐ 4-3 ***Poor Planning:*** I feel so bad about myself that I can't make realistic plans. Sometimes I make grandiose plans and try to do more than is possible. At other times I sell myself short by planning to do too little, because I don't believe in myself. At still other times I don't make any plans at all. I refuse to think about what I'm going to do next. I interpret the slogan "One Day at a Time" to mean that I shouldn't plan ahead or think about what I'm going to do next. My plans are based more on wishful thinking (how I wish things would be) than on reality (how things actually are).

☐ 4-4 ***Plans Begin to Fail:*** My plans begin to fail and each failure causes new problems. I tend to over-react to or mismanage each problem in a way that creates a new and bigger problem. I start having the same kinds of problems with work, friends, family, and money that I used to have before I got into recovery. I feel guilty and remorseful when I have these problems. I work hard to try to solve them, but something always seems to go wrong that creates an even bigger or more depressing problem.

Stop reading and take a moment to identify one of the warning signs that you've just read that stood out to you most.

1. Which warning sign stood out to you? _____

    _____

2. Why did it stand out? _____

    _____

Phase 5: Immobilization

During this phase I feel trapped in an endless stream of unmanageable problems and feel like giving up. I can't seem to get started or make myself do the things that I know I need to do. Even when I try, nothing seems to work out. The most common relapse warning signs are:

☐ 5-1 *Daydreaming and Wishful Thinking:* It becomes more difficult to concentrate or figure things out. I have fantasies of escaping or "being rescued from it all" by an event that's unlikely to happen. I start daydreaming and wishing that I could get the things that I want without having to do anything to get them. I want something magical to happen that will rescue me from it all.

□ 5-2 *Feeling that Nothing Can Be Solved:* I begin to feel like a failure who will never be able to get anything right. My failures may be real or imagined. I exaggerate small problems and blow them out of proportion while failing to notice anything that I do right. I start to believe that "I've tried my best and recovery isn't working out."

□ 5-3 *Immature Wish to Be Happy:* I have a vague desire to "be happy" or to have "things work out," but I don't set up any plans to make those things happen. I want to be happy, but I have no idea what I can do to make myself happy. I'm not willing to work hard or pay the price for the happiness that I want. I start wishing that something magical would happen to rescue me from my problems.

Stop reading and take a moment to identify one of the warning signs that you've just read that stood out to you most.

1. Which warning sign stood out to you?_____

_____

2. Why did it stand out? _____

_____

Phase 6: Confusion and Overreaction

I have trouble thinking clearly and managing my thoughts, feelings, and actions. I'm irritable and I tend to overreact to small things. The most common relapse warning signs are:

☐ 6-1 *Difficulty in Thinking Clearly:* I have trouble thinking clearly and solving simple problems. Sometimes my mind races and I can't shut it off, and at other times it seems to shut off or go blank. My mind tends to wander and I have difficulty thinking about something for more than a few minutes. I get confused and have trouble figuring out how one thing relates to or affects other things. I also have difficulty deciding what to do next in order to manage my life and recovery. As a result I tend to make bad decisions that I wouldn't have made if I were thinking clearly.

☐ 6-2 *Difficulty in Managing Feelings and Emotions:* I start to have difficulty managing my feelings and emotions. Sometimes I overreact emotionally and feel too much. At other times I become emotionally numb and can't figure out what I'm feeling. Sometimes I feel strange or have "crazy feelings" for no apparent reason. I start to think I might be going crazy. I have strong mood swings and periodically feel depressed, anxious, and scared. As a result of this, I don't trust my feelings and emotions and often try to ignore, stuff, or forget about them. My mood sweeps start causing me new problems.

☐ 6-3 *Difficulty Remembering Things:* At times I have problems remembering things and learning new information and skills. Things I want to remember seem to dissolve or evaporate from my mind within minutes. I also have problems remembering key events from my childhood, adolescence, or adulthood. At times I remember things clearly, but at other times these same memories won't come to mind. I feel blocked, stuck, or cut off from these memories. At times, my inability to remember things causes me to make bad decisions that I wouldn't have made if my memory were working properly.

☐ 6-4 *Periods of Confusion:* I start getting confused more often. The confusion is more severe and lasts longer. I'm not sure what's right or wrong. I don't know what to do to solve my problems, because everything I try seems to make them worse. I get angry at myself, because I can't solve my problems and I just keep making things worse.

☐ 6-5 *Difficulty Managing Stress:* I start having trouble dealing with stress. Sometimes I feel numb and can't recognize the minor signs of daily stress. At other times I seem overwhelmed by severe stress for no real reason. When I feel stressed out, I can't relax no matter what I do. The things other people do to relax either don't work for me or they make the stress worse. It seems I get so tense that I'm not in control. The stress starts to get so bad that I can't do the things I normally do. I get afraid that I'll collapse physically or emotionally.

☐ 6-6 *Irritation with Friends:* My relationships with friends, family, counselors, and other recovering people become strained. Sometimes I feel threat-

ened when others talk about the changes they're
noticing in my behavior and moods. At other times
I just don't care about what they say. The arguments
and conflicts get worse in spite of my efforts to re-
solve them. I start to feel guilty.

□ 6-7   *Easily Angered:* I feel irritable and frustrated. I
start losing my temper for no real reason and feeling guilty afterwards. I often overreact to small
things that really shouldn't make any difference. I
start avoiding people because I'm afraid I might
lose control and get violent. The effort to control
myself adds to the stress and tension.

Stop reading and take a moment to identify one of the
warning signs that you've just read that stood out to you
most.

1.   Which warning sign stood out to you?_____

   _____

2.   Why did it stand out? _____

   _____

Phase 7:   Depression

During this phase, I become so depressed that I can't do
the things I normally do. At times I feel that life is not worth
living, and sometimes I think about killing myself or relapsing as a way to end the depression. I'm so depressed that I
can't hide it from others. The most common relapse warning signs are:

☐ 7-1 **Irregular Eating Habits:** Either I start to overeat or I lose my appetite and eat very little. As a result I start gaining or losing weight. I skip meals and stop eating at regular times. I replace a well-balanced, nourishing diet with "junk food."

☐ 7-2 **Lack of Desire to Take Action:** I can't get started or get anything done. At those times I'm unable to concentrate; I feel anxious, fearful, and uneasy. I often feel trapped, with no way out.

☐ 7-3 **Difficulty Sleeping Restfully:** I have difficulty sleeping restfully. I can't fall asleep. When I do sleep, I have unusual or disturbing dreams, awaken many times, and have difficulty falling back to sleep. I sleep fitfully and rarely experience a deep, relaxing sleep. I wake up from a night of sleep feeling tired. The times of day during which I sleep change. At times, I stay up late due to an inability to fall asleep, and then oversleep because I'm too tired to get up in the morning. At times I become so exhausted that I sleep for extremely long periods, sometimes sleeping around the clock for one or more days.

☐ 7-4 **Loss of Daily Structure:** My daily routine becomes haphazard. I stop getting up and going to bed at regular times. I start skipping meals and eating at unusual times. I find it hard to keep appointments and plan social events. I feel rushed and overburdened at times and then have nothing to do at other times. I'm unable to follow through on plans and decisions, and I experience tension, frustration, fear, and anxiety that keep me from doing what I know needs to be done.

☐ 7-5 **_Periods of Deep Depression:_** I feel depressed more often. The depression becomes worse, lasts longer, and interferes with living. The depression is so bad that it's noticed by others and can't be easily denied. The depression is most severe during unplanned or unstructured periods of time. Fatigue, hunger, and loneliness make the depression worse. When I feel depressed, I separate from other people, become irritable and angry with others, and often complain that nobody cares or understands what I'm going through.

Stop reading and take a moment to identify one of the warning signs that you've just read that stood out to you most.

1.   Which warning sign stood out to you?_____

   _____

2.   Why did it stand out? _____

   _____

Phase 8:   Loss of Control

I can't control my thoughts, feelings, or behaviors. My life becomes so unmanageable that I start to believe there are only three ways out—insanity, suicide, or relapse. I no longer believe that anyone or anything can help me. The most common warning signs are:

☐ 8-1 **_Hiding My Problems:_** I feel guilty because I believe I'm doing things wrong. I hide my problems and stop telling others what's happening to me. The more I hide my problems, the worse they get.

☐ 8-2 **_Feeling Powerless and Helpless:_** I start to believe that there's nothing I can do to handle my problems in recovery. I make up my mind to get back on track and try to do things differently, but I fall back into the same patterns of dysfunctional behavior. I have trouble getting started. I have difficulty thinking clearly and paying attention to things. I start to believe that I can't do anything right and that there's no way out. I feel sorry for myself and use self-pity to get attention from others. I feel ashamed, crazy, and defective. I don't believe I'll ever feel normal again.

☐ 8-3 **_Refusing Help:_** I avoid talking with people who care about me and want to help me. Sometimes I drive them away by getting angry and criticizing them. At other times I quietly withdraw from them. I feel helpless and start to lose respect for myself. I have no confidence that I can do anything to solve my problems. I try to hide these feelings by acting as if I don't care.

☐ 8-4 **_Breaking My Recovery Program:_** I find excuses to miss scheduled recovery activities because they don't make me feel better. I start to tell myself that I don't have to keep my recovery program as a number-one priority. Other things seem more important. Eventually I stop attending all scheduled recovery activities, even though I need help and I know it.

☐ 8-5 **_Going against My Values:_** I begin to do things that I believe are wrong. I know that I'm lying, using denial, and making excuses for my behavior, but I can't stop myself. I feel out of control. I start doing things on a regular basis that I normally wouldn't do, things that violate my values. I just can't seem to stop myself or control my behavior.

☐ 8-6 **_Complete Loss of Self-Confidence:_** I feel trapped and overwhelmed because I can't think clearly or do the things that I know I need to do to solve my problems. I feel powerless and hopeless. I start to believe that I'm useless and incompetent, and that I'll never be able to manage my life.

☐ 8-7 **_Unreasonable Resentment:_** I feel angry because of my inability to behave the way I want to. Sometimes my anger is with the world in general, sometimes with someone or something in particular, and sometimes with myself.

☐ 8-8 **_Overwhelming Loneliness, Frustration, Anger, and Tension:_** I feel completely overwhelmed. I feel like I'm helpless, desperate, and about to go crazy. It keeps getting harder and harder to control my thoughts, feelings, and behavior. My problems keep getting worse. No matter how hard I try to get back in control, I can't do it.

Stop reading and take a moment to identify one of the warning signs that you've just read that stood out to you most.

1. Which warning sign stood out to you?_____

   _____

2. Why did it stand out? _____

   _____

Phase 9: Thinking about Relapse

I start to think that relapsing will help me solve my problems and feel better. Things seem so bad that I begin to think I might as well relapse because things couldn't get worse. I want to believe that I can have a short-term, low-consequence relapse without experiencing major problems, even though deep inside I know I can't. I try to put these thoughts out of my mind, but sometimes they're so strong that I can't stop them. I start to believe that relapsing is the only way to keep myself from going crazy or killing myself. It actually looks like a sane and rational alternative.

☐ 9-1 *Thinking about Relapse:* I start hoping that I can be normal and not have to worry about working a recovery program. I imagine what it would be like if I could go back to my old way of doing things without experiencing any pain or problems. I start to think that a relapse will help me feel better. I start to believe I might really be able to control it next time.

☐ 9-2 *Getting Dissatisfied with Recovery:* I look at my recovery and notice all of the pain and problems I'm experiencing. Things seem so bad that I begin to think that I might as well relapse because things couldn't get any worse. Life seems to have become unmanageable even though I'm in recovery.

☐ 9-3 *Getting Obsessed with Relapse:* The thoughts about relapse keep popping into my head. Sometimes I'm able to put these thoughts out of my mind, but often they're so strong that I can't stop them. I begin to believe that relapsing is the only alternative to going crazy or committing suicide. Relapsing actually looks like a sane and rational alternative, and I can't stop thinking about it.

☐ 9-4 **Convincing Myself to Relapse:** I mistakenly believe that relapsing will somehow make my problems better or allow me to escape from them for a little while. I tell myself that the relapse will be controlled and time-limited. I think about relapsing, getting relief, and then getting back into recovery before I lose control.

Stop reading and take a moment to identify one of the warning signs that you've just read that stood out to you most.

1. Which warning sign stood out to you?_____

     _____

2. Why did it stand out? _____

     _____

Phase 10:   Relapse

I start the relapse and try to control it. I feel disappointed because the relapse isn't doing for me what I thought it would. I feel guilty because I know that I mismanaged my recovery. My relapse spirals out of control, creating severe problems with my life and health. The problems continue to get worse until I realize that I need help and decide to try recovery one more time.

□ 10-1 ***Starting the Relapse:*** I try to solve my problems and feel better by relapsing. Although I try to rationalize my behavior, deep inside I know that the relapse won't work and that it will hurt me in the long run. I convince myself that I have no choice. I try to tell myself that relapsing is a normal behavior and that I can handle it this time.

□ 10-2 ***Attempting to Control:*** I try to focus on the positive aspects of the relapse and keep the problems under control. I convince myself that I feel better when I'm using my relapse behaviors. I deny or block out the pain and problems caused by the relapse. I start moving in and out of various self-destructive behaviors related to the relapse. I convince myself that I can handle it.

□ 10-3 ***Feeling Disappointed:*** I feel disappointed because the relapse isn't doing for me what I thought it would. I feel guilty because I believe I've done something wrong. I feel ashamed because I start to believe that I'm defective and worthless as a person and my relapse proves it.

□ 10-4 ***Loss of Control:*** My relapse spirals out of control. At times I feel that I can handle it, and then I lose it and get into trouble. I try to control again and start to cycle in and out of the problems caused by the relapse. I feel the relapse gathering momentum and I can see that I'm losing control. Sometimes I lose control slowly. At other times, the loss of control is very rapid. No matter how hard I try, I can't stop and get back into recovery.

□ 10-5 ***Life and Health Problems:*** I start having severe problems with my life and health. Marriage, jobs, and friendships are seriously damaged. Eventually, I hit a crisis that forces me to seek treatment and start all over again.

Stop reading and take a moment to identify one of the warning signs that you've just read that stood out to you most.

1. Which warning sign stood out to you?_____

_____

2. Why did it stand out? _____

_____

Chapter 10

CENAPS Brief Warning Signs List

The following list of warning signs was also developed by Terence T. Gorski and is a modification of the original list of thirty-seven warning signs. They provide a brief overview of the original list, summarizing the relapse process from stable recovery to relapse. They can be used in a session with your therapist, sponsor, or support group. Read the following warning signs and identify those that stand out most for you.

1. Internal Change

I start using old ways of thinking, managing feelings, and behaving that make me look good on the outside but leave me feeling bad on the inside. I get more stressed than usual, and my recovery program seems less important. My moods swing from feeling on top of the world to feeling like nothing is working out. Deep inside I start to feel like something is wrong, but I try to cover it up.

2. Denial

I stop paying attention to or honestly telling others what I'm thinking and feeling. I start worrying about the changes in my thinking, feelings, and behavior. I don't want to think about it or talk about it. I go into denial and try to convince myself that everything is OK when I know it really isn't.

3. Avoidance and Defensiveness

I avoid people who will honestly point out the problems I don't want to see. When they do, I get defensive, scared, and angry. I blame them for making me feel bad. I take the focus off myself by criticizing their problems and faults instead of honestly looking at my own problems. I start using compulsive behaviors to keep my mind off how uncomfortable I'm feeling. I start creating problems for myself by using poor judgment and impulsively doing things without thinking them through. I start feeling uncomfortable around others, spend more time alone, and start to feel lonely and isolated.

4. Crisis Building

I start having problems that I don't understand. Even though I want to solve these problems and I work hard at it, two new problems pop up to replace every problem I solve. I can't see the big picture, and I start doing things that won't really help. I start to feel depressed and try to distract myself by getting busy with other things and not talking about the depression. I stop planning ahead. Things keep going wrong, and I feel like nothing is going my way. No matter how hard I try, nothing seems to work.

5. Immobilization

I feel trapped in an endless stream of unmanageable problems. I get tired of putting time and energy into things that aren't working. I feel like giving up. I can't seem to get started or make myself do the things that I know I need to do. I exaggerate small problems and blow them out of proportion. I can't force myself to deal with the major things that could really make a difference. I begin to feel like a failure who can't do anything right. I start wishing I could run away or that something magical would happen to rescue me from my problems.

6. Confusion and Overreaction

I have trouble thinking clearly and solving usually simple problems. Sometimes my mind races and I can't shut it off. At other times I go blank and can't concentrate on anything. I have trouble remembering things. I switch from overreacting to feeling emotionally numb. I start to think that I might be going crazy. I stop trusting my feelings and try to ignore, stuff, or forget about them. I start making bad decisions that I wouldn't have made if I were thinking clearly. I become easily angered and start to take it out on my friends and family. I get irritated with other people because they don't understand me and can't seem to help me.

7. Depression

I get so depressed that I can't do the things I normally do. I feel that life is not worth living, and sometimes I think about killing myself or relapsing as a way to end the depression. I'm so depressed that I can't hide it from others. I stop eating right. I can't get started or get anything done. I sleep fitfully and rarely experience a deep, relaxing sleep. I can't stick to a productive daily schedule. I find it hard to keep appointments and plan ahead. I isolate myself and convince myself that nobody cares and that there's no one who can help me. I feel trapped, with no way out.

8. Loss of Control

I start doing things that violate my values, hurt me, and hurt those I love. As a result, I start losing respect for myself. I find excuses to miss my therapy and self-help group meetings. I cut myself off from others by ignoring them, getting angry with them, or criticizing and putting them down. I get so isolated that it seems there's no one to turn to for help. I start to feel sorry for myself and use self-pity to get attention. I feel ashamed and guilty. I know that I'm out of control but I keep lying, using denial, and making excuses for my behavior. I feel trapped by the pain and start to believe that I'll never be able to manage my life. I see only three possible ways out: insanity, suicide, or relapse. I no longer believe that anyone or anything else can help me. No matter how hard I try to regain control, I'm unable to do so.

9. Thinking about Relapse

I start to think that having a relapse will help me solve my problems and feel better. Things seem so bad that I begin to think I might as well relapse because things couldn't get worse. I try to convince myself that I can use relapse behaviors without losing control or developing serious problems, even though deep down inside I know I can't. I try to put these thoughts about relapse out of my mind, but sometimes they're so strong I can't stop them. I start to believe that relapsing is the only way to keep myself from going crazy or killing myself. Relapsing actually looks like a sane and rational alternative.

10. Relapse

I try to solve my problems and feel better by relapsing. Although I rationalize my behavior, deep inside I know that relapsing won't work and will hurt me in the long run. I start the relapse and try to control my behavior. I feel myself losing control and get disappointed because the relapse isn't doing for me what I thought it would. My relapse spirals out of control, creating severe problems with my life and health. The problems continue to get worse until I realize that I need help and decide to try recovery one more time.

Chapter 11

Relapse Warning Signs for African Americans

The following list addresses relapse issues that frequently occur for African Americans. It is important to note that most of these twenty-two warning signs are rooted in real conditions of racism and oppression. They should not be dismissed summarily as insignificant ploys by clients to avoid dealing with their addiction. They often began with a legitimate concern stemming from a real or perceived injustice. They become relapse issues when they get distorted and are used as an excuse to drink, use, or otherwise reject recovery. These real problems can be used by the client to sabotage recovery. So consider these warning signs as a starting point. You and the client can begin to explore what may be the driving force behind each warning sign. The goal is to identify a place where you can begin to discuss and eventually manage these warning signs.

The client should read the list of twenty-two warning signs. After reading each warning sign, pause for a moment and notice your thoughts and feelings. Put a check mark next to any warning sign that has been experienced. Put a question mark next to any warning sign that is difficult to understand. Underline any word or phrase that stands out.

Clients should be prepared to discuss this with their counselor, group members, and/or recovery sponsor.

1. Can I be black and still be in recovery?

I sometimes feel like I'm not acting, talking, or associating the way a black person should. I feel like I don't talk or behave "black" enough and I begin to feel like a "sell out." I've changed many behaviors because of my recovery and therefore get accused of turning into a "square." I'm using less slang and trying to improve my grammar, but I don't want to abandon my culture. Sometimes I'm not sure what exactly my culture is. I want to improve myself but stay connected to my roots. I don't want to appear like I'm trying to be better than anyone, but I don't want to live the way I used to. I want and need the acceptance of my people *and* to grow as a human being. I don't want to be called an "Uncle Tom" or a "square" just because I'm starting to change my life. Sometimes my friends accuse me of trying to be "too good for them," and I don't know how to separate from them to protect my recovery and still feel OK with myself. Many times I feel like I'm two different people: one my recovery self and one my black self. I argue with myself and don't always know the right thing to do. I get confused and frustrated and sometimes begin to act in old self-defeating ways just to fit in and appear more black.

2. It's because I'm black.

I think that most of the bad things that happen in my life are because I'm black. I feel confident that nonblacks do not have to go through the misery and oppression we blacks endure on a regular basis. I start to feel like the reason people treat me so poorly is because I'm black. The problems I have in my job, school, and society are primarily because I'm black. I can feel it at meetings, too. I'm not as accepted as the nonblacks and it makes me uncomfortable. I get singled out for negative treatment based solely on my race. I always seem to get the short end of the deal. Even when I'm in public conducting business, I can tell that I'm being treated differently. I get poor and often rude service just because I'm black. I get angry and distrustful and want to either strike out or run away.

3. Nobody knows the trouble I've seen.

I feel like nobody really knows and understands how hard it is for me. I feel like the only people who may have a clue are other black folks, but even most of them don't fully realize how truly difficult my life is. I feel overwhelmed and pessimistic. I often feel like it's me against the world and that there is no way I can succeed. I feel like damaged goods and nobody really wants me around. I've harmed myself and a lot of other people, and my life is a mess. I want to be in recovery but it's too hard for me and I probably won't make it anyway—I'm too far gone. I feel like giving up and I stop trying to make my recovery work.

4. I deserve better than this.

When the slaves were freed they were promised forty acres and a mule. I still haven't got mine. Society owes me something; after the years of racism and oppression that my people have had to endure, there should be some payback. I start to feel like I've got something coming to me. I feel like I should get special treatment to make up for all the years of bad treatment black people have received. I find myself acting in ways that suggest that I don't have to follow all the rules. I want people to get off my back. I feel different and unique and get accused of having a "chip on my shoulder." I feel like the world owes me an apology, and I easily get angry when people minimize my situation.

Sometimes people treat me as though I should be grateful that slavery no longer exists. They act as though everything is fine now, but I know that it is not. I get resentful and argumentative and don't bother to try to explain myself to most people because they won't understand. I do what I want to do, when I want to do it, and I don't worry about the consequences.

5. If you're black, get back.

There is an old saying: "If you're white, you're all right. If you're brown, stick around. But if you're black, get back...get back...get back." I feel "less than" because of my race—a second-class citizen. I start to focus on things in society that suggest blacks are bad or inferior. I notice that even among other blacks I judge them by the color of their skin—the lighter the better. I have negative opinions about kinky hair and thick noses and lips. I find myself going to nonblack businesses because I believe they will be superior to black businesses. I fantasize or get into romantic relationships with nonblacks because I tell myself they are higher quality. I judge my own success and progress by how far I've come away from my black roots. I avoid associating with blacks who I feel are too stereotypical. I become part of the racism that exists within the black community and find myself being prejudiced against my own people. I feel either better than or less than, even within my own race. I start to believe whites are better than me just because of their race. I either resent them or seek their approval and acceptance. Sometimes I do both.

6. I have to work twice as hard just to be in the game.

I feel that because I'm black I have to do more than everyone else just to be treated like an equal. I feel a lot of pressure to perform and produce. I sometimes think others are waiting for me to fail, so I try extra hard to prove myself. I find myself trying to disprove the myths and stereotypes of black people being lazy and inadequate. I act as though I'm representing the whole black race and want to make a good impression. I wonder sometimes if I'm trying to overcompensate for my insecurity. I don't feel valued unless I do more than everyone else. Sometimes I feel unworthy and ashamed and tend to cover that up by trying to be superhuman. I have had to overcome many obstacles, and many situations feel like a contest to me. I compete with my coworkers and friends and am hypersensitive to criticism. I feel burned-out and stressed and don't always take good care of myself. I tend to overwork and spend so much time trying to succeed that I rarely have time to relax. My eating and sleeping habits are not very healthy. I need a vacation but I feel so driven that I can't stop.

7. I'm only comfortable around my own people.

I feel uncomfortable around nonblacks. I don't feel like I belong with them and don't feel they can relate to me and my issues. I certainly don't relate to them and their issues. I even feel uneasy around some blacks, mostly those who didn't drink or use the way I did. I know I have a lot of trouble trusting people and always notice when people are faking. I focus on differences rather than similarities and have a hard time connecting with others. I spend most of my time with just a few people, mostly other blacks with similar backgrounds. Even in meetings I gravitate toward the other blacks in the fellowship and avoid developing relationships with nonblacks. I avoid nonblacks and discourage them from being friends with me. I am selective about who I associate with, and my circle of support is not very large. I do not share my feelings or recovery issues with people outside my support system, and because my support system is so small most people don't know me very well. I resist taking risks and getting to know others and don't really believe it is worth the effort. I feel like it would be too much work and I don't see the value. I feel fine where I am and don't want to change.

8. So what's wrong with being cool?

I can't help it if I'm cool. I enjoy being a "player." I think that people wish they had what I have. I want people to know I'm not a square and that I'm in the "game." I refuse to change my mannerisms because I don't think there is anything wrong with the way I am—others are jealous. I don't think people in recovery really understand and honor my individuality. Others judge me, but that's their business. I am who I am. I use a lot of slang and profanity because that's my language. People accuse me of acting and talking like I'm on the streets and try to get me to change but I resist. I've been told that I have an attitude problem, and many people seem to be intimidated by me. Occasionally I do get in trouble with my ways. I think of committing crimes to make fast money or conning people in recovery. Whenever I try to be different and more mainstream it feels weird and phony, and I always find myself going back to old ways. Sometimes I don't think I'm cut out for recovery and I miss the way it used to be. I believe that I'm addicted to the old lifestyle of drinking, using, and hustling.

9. I have been hurt by racism.

I have been the victim of racism. I have had people call me names and treat me unfairly because of my race. I have been in situations where I feel nervous or afraid of what someone will think or do. I know racist people who dislike or hate me because I'm black. I feel threatened and discriminated against. It's unfair and unjust and I'm angry. I notice that my feelings get hurt deeply when I'm the victim of racism and I want to completely avoid the person responsible. I don't always feel safe even in recovery. I have heard my nonblack "friends" in recovery tell racist jokes or make rude comments and I'm offended and uncomfortable. When I experience racism in recovery I get very sad and disillusioned and think it's all a waste of time. Sometimes I think all people are prejudiced against black folks but just don't admit it. I never forgive people once I find out they are racist.

10. I can be a racist, too.

I have been the perpetrator of racism. I call people names and treat them unfairly because of their race. I have hurt or scared people intentionally because of their race. I tease and discount people and say rude and insensitive things to people because of their race. I notice that I am prejudiced and have many negative, preconceived notions about other races. I tell jokes about other races and put them down. I can be mean and treat them harshly if they get in my way. Sometimes I find myself intentionally being threatening and aggressive to people, hoping to instigate a fight. I don't like some races and I have strong negative feelings that I won't try to hide. I don't like to mingle with other races and I feel that they are the enemy. I have difficulty in recovery because of my racist views and feelings.

11. I like being the only black in the group.

I prefer and seek out the company of nonblacks. I find myself being the only black in my group, and I work hard to keep it that way. Even though it's occasionally uncomfortable, I feel accepted—so I stay. I am resistant to other blacks entering my world because it feels like they are intruding. I notice that I'm territorial regarding these nonblack people and seem to get much of my self-worth from their approval. Sometimes I feel like they don't really like me for who I am; they just want me around because I'm black. I think they just want to be able to say they have a black friend. I have heard my nonblack friends tell racist jokes around me or make rude comments and I pretend that it doesn't bother me. I have been told that I don't act or seem like most black folks; that feels strange but I accept it as a compliment. Sometimes in my role as the token black I act like the "entertainer" for the crowd—singing, dancing, and even telling jokes about my own people. I've gotten so used to being in this world it is difficult for me to be around many black people. Sometimes I feel like a traitor, but mostly I feel like I have a better life.

12. I knew it all along.

I believe that most people are closet racists, and I spend a lot of my time watching and waiting for them to slip up so I can expose them. I am very sensitive to racist comments and tend to think people say a lot of things without thinking. Sometimes I misunderstand someone and make a mistake, but usually I'm right. I get offended easily and tend to hold grudges. I'm very guarded and suspicious— people have to prove themselves to me before I trust them. My support system does not consist of many nonblacks. I have difficulty relaxing around most people, and even in meetings I'm tense. I rarely get my hopes up because I know people will let me down. I'm sad and lonely a lot and don't have much faith in humankind. I've never been good at surrendering and "turning it over" because I hate being powerless. Some people say I have control issues but I feel that it's just self-preservation. Some people say I'm cynical but I think I'm just realistic. Most of the time I feel bitter and angry.

13. I shouldn't act too black.

I was taught as a child that being black was a handicap. I find myself apologizing to the world for my blackness and trying real hard to not rock the boat. I feel embarrassed when I see other blacks acting ignorant and unsophisticated. I associate many of my natural instincts with negativity. I tone down my dress, speech, and behavior so it won't appear so black. When I get angry or uncomfortable I notice that I "relapse" into blackness, and it can scare people. Intellectually I know that there's nothing wrong with being black, but I can't turn off the old tapes that tell me being black is bad and makes me "less than." Sometimes I feel confused and frustrated.

14. I don't stand up enough for my culture.

I feel like I have to accommodate other cultures even when I would rather say or do something that's more consistent with my culture. I tend to minimize my own cultural needs so I won't make others uncomfortable. I support others' right to celebrate and flaunt their cultural beliefs, but I do not feel supported in return. I feel pressure to avoid situations that might concern others and resist conflict even if it means denying myself something I want to do or say. I am always aware that my blackness and my fellowship with other blacks may make some people nervous, so I try to assure them that everything is fine. I feel the need to take care of my nonblack friends and prevent them from becoming confused, afraid, or left out. I feel resentment sometimes because I don't feel like it is acceptable for me to be my black self. Even with my taste in clothes, jewelry, hairstyle, music, and language, I feel I must be careful so I don't make others feel uncomfortable. I find myself trying to control the situation by being very aggressive and dominant or I give my power away. In both cases I wind up more concerned with others' needs than my own.

15. My sexual behavior can sabotage my recovery.

I believe the myth is true. I feel I must prove to the world what a good sexual partner I am. Much of my self-esteem comes from my ability to be good in bed. I notice that I don't feel good about myself if I'm not sexually active. It's very important for me that others find me sexually attractive and desirable. When I'm in a relationship I use sex for power and I have urges to be unfaithful. I find myself in multiple sexual relationships and I have a hard time saying no. I use poor judgment when it comes to sex and often have sex with the wrong people. I know that my recovery has been threatened by my sexual behavior but I can't seem to stop. I think about sex all the time and have lied and manipulated to have sex. Sometimes I crave sex so much that I have difficulty concentrating. Even when I don't have a sexual partner, much of my time and energy is spent on sexual fantasy and pursuit. I know that I use sex to fix and believe that it may be an addiction for me. I know that I sometimes confuse sex with love. I need to feel loved and sex is a quick way to get that feeling. I have allowed myself to be used and I've used others. I often feel guilty and empty after sex.

16. I'm working myself to death.

I seem to be driven by my desire to achieve success. I work long hours trying to be successful. I am often tired and frustrated by the end of the week. Some people call me a workaholic—and they may be right. I get so busy with my work that I don't always have time for my recovery. I don't eat and rest like I should and rarely take time off from work. I measure my success by my possessions. I keep trying to get more and more material things to prove I'm a success. I never have enough. I want a bigger house, a nicer car, and more expensive clothes. I keep thinking that I should be satisfied but I never am. I believe in the American Dream but I don't know if it is a reality for black folks. No matter how much I have I still feel like a second-class citizen.

17. I'm so angry.

Sometimes I feel like a time bomb. I have a lot of anger inside me—and with good reason! I am angry about all the struggles I have just because I'm black. I'm angry that the world isn't fair and that I get treated differently. I seem to always have a fire burning inside me. I have to be careful because when I get mad I may lose control. Sometimes I take my anger out on the wrong person and then I feel bad. I stuff my feelings and usually don't talk about my anger and resentment until it gets to be overwhelming. When I get angry with someone in recovery I find it hard to let go; I hold grudges and have thoughts of violence. When I'm feeling angry with myself for my addiction and all the mistakes I've made in life, I get real self-destructive. It doesn't take much for my anger to turn to rage. It's hard for me to be spiritual when I am consumed with this rage.

18. Don't tell me what to do.

I resist authority figures and sometimes treat them like the enemy. I feel like black people have been bossed around for too many years. I am tired of taking orders and have a real hard time with anybody telling me what to do. I have problems with my sponsor, supervisor, and counselor. I especially have problems with nonblacks in positions of authority. I don't trust them and think they are trying to put me down or be better than me. I know that I have to "surrender" and "turn it over" in recovery, but it's hard for me because I don't feel safe when other people are in charge. Sometimes when I'm told to do something I do just the opposite. I have a hard time following directions. I want people to know they can't control me.

19. I don't date other blacks.

I want only the best in life—and it ain't black. I don't date other blacks and don't find them attractive. I think other races are more attractive and desirable than my own. I use my blackness to "catch." They like me because I'm black and I like them because they're not. When I'm with my nonblack partner, I feel superior to other blacks and think they must be jealous. It is a boost to my ego when I can have a partner who is nonblack. Somehow I've come to believe that black is not good enough for me.

20. I wish people weren't so afraid of me.

People lock their car doors and clutch their purses when I approach. When I go into a store the security guard follows me around. People look at me with suspicion and fear. If something comes up missing and I'm around I always seem to be the first suspect. I know this is a reaction to my blackness and it makes me angry and uncomfortable. I can't change the way I look and I'm tired of being treated like a monster or criminal. I feel powerless, sad, and lonely.

21. I can't betray my family.

I am very connected to my family even though many of them are not good for my recovery. I have been told that I must stay out of slippery places and avoid people who use or sell drugs, but it's hard for me when it's my family. It's difficult for me to imagine not being around my family but I don't know if I can stay clean and sober if I keep going back to them. I am very confused about this. My family isn't perfect but neither am I, and I feel like I'm being disloyal if I try to separate from them. Some members of my family support my recovery but others think it's a waste of time and almost seem to be trying to sabotage my sobriety. I often feel like the responsibility I have for my family is stronger than the responsibility I have for myself and my recovery. Sometimes I feel like my family needs me and I need them, and because I don't think I can have both them and recovery, I decide recovery may not work for me.

22. I have a spiritual dilemma.

I have much shame and guilt about my life as an addict. I feel like I have let my Higher Power down, and I have difficulty letting go of that feeling of failure. I was raised as a spiritual person and I know who my God is. I feel like I knew better and I can't forget or forgive myself for some of the things I did. I'm having problems reconnecting spiritually and sometimes wonder if I will ever get back to the way I used to be.

Sometimes when I do feel connected with my Higher Power I put all my faith in spiritual practices and neglect my other support systems. I wind up associating primarily with people who understand me spiritually but have no idea of my life as an addict. They give me advice on how to get closer to God but they don't have much insight into my disease. I try really hard to deal with the cravings, obsessions, and other drug-related feelings and thoughts in church or prayer but something seems to be missing. Sometimes I'm ashamed to say what's really on my mind because it won't sound right and I don't think these people would understand. I often feel guilty and "dirty" about some of my thoughts, feelings, and actions. I feel like an impostor.

I get angry at meetings or around other recovering people when I feel like they don't understand or accept my Higher

Power. The concept that your Higher Power can be any-thing—"even a doorknob"—bothers me. Sometimes I don't feel like it's OK for me to be honest about my God in meet-ings without people having a negative reaction. Sometimes I think meetings might not be the best thing for me and I want to stop going.

Chapter 12

Underlying Recovery Issues

Let's now talk about the warning signs in a little more detail. Each of these twenty-two warning signs contains several underlying recovery issues. These issues are probably consistent with all chemical dependency clients regardless of race. However, the ways a black client might experience the underlying issues are different, as illustrated in the warning signs. For example, a black client experiencing fear and low self-esteem will probably cite racism as a factor. A white client most likely will not. Yet in both cases you must deal with a client who has fear and low self-esteem. Race is actually secondary to the clinical issues at hand.

It makes sense to familiarize yourself with the underlying issues related to each warning sign. I suggest also that you be vigilant in attempting to get to the "core" recovery issue of each warning sign. This will demystify the warning sign and give the clinician and the client a place to begin work. It will be easier to work on a recovery theme that both client and clinician are familiar with. For example, denial, rationalization, and manipulation are issues that can be identified and processed quickly and effectively. By focusing on the underlying recovery theme, the clinician can stay on task and keep the client moving in the right direction.

Keeping this in mind will probably save the client and the clinician hours of time spent in a guarded and uncomfortable gridlock.

I will briefly discuss the dynamics that drive each warning sign. These descriptions are not absolute. They are based on my experience and that of others who have contributed to this work. However, your client may have a totally different experience and process related to a warning sign. Validate that experience; don't try to insist that it be as it is written here. At the end of each description is a cluster of recovery issues that might be at the core of the warning sign. By identifying the core issues you will be in a better position to process the thoughts, feelings, and actions with the client.

1. Can I be black and still be in recovery?

This warning sign describes the conflict many blacks feel when they try to change and improve themselves. There is some confusion about how a "real" black person talks and behaves. Sometimes there is pressure to behave and speak in a certain style that lends itself to slang and illiteracy. Many blacks feel guilty and disloyal that they aren't acting or speaking "black" enough. Most blacks will describe feeling bilingual (i.e., able to communicate in two languages: "black English" and "white English"). Often blacks will experience pressure and ridicule from friends and family when they begin to change their behavior, mannerisms, speech, and associates. They might be accused of "selling out" their blackness. The client experiencing this warning sign will probably display guilt, confusion, and resentment.

Underlying Recovery Issues: Fear of change, pressure, high-risk situation, guilt, awkwardness, discomfort, people-pleasing, shame, anxiety, confusion.

2. It's because I'm black.

This warning sign describes the dynamic of victimization. Many blacks honestly believe that most of the bad things that happen to them happen because they're black. Often this is reinforced by some real situation of discrimination. They use that situation as proof that the world is against them because they are black. This belief can sabotage recovery when it prevents clients from taking responsibility for their actions and quality of life. Clients experiencing this warning sign will often have difficulty identifying their own issues and will express much denial.

Underlying Recovery Issues: Blaming, projecting, victimizing, self-pity, refusal to accept responsibility for one's own actions, denial, justification, entitlement.

3. Nobody knows the trouble I've seen.

This warning sign describes a deep sense of loneliness and self-pity. Life has been very hard for many blacks, and they often genuinely feel that no one understands what it's like to walk in their shoes. They feel isolated and without viable resources. They feel they must do most things on their own, without help from others. Many blacks have unfortunately developed a tolerance for intolerable conditions. Pessimism and hopelessness are precursors for the depression many blacks feel. Clients experiencing this warning sign will probably not seek help willingly and will have little faith about their chances for recovery.

Underlying Recovery Issues: Self-pity, pessimism, hopelessness, depression, being overwhelmed, exclusion, stagnation.

4. I deserve better than this.

This warning sign describes a sense of entitlement. When the slaves were freed they were promised "forty acres and a mule." That promise never came true. That broken promise is symbolic of the deprivation and entitlement many blacks feel. Many blacks feel that society has historically and consistently "wronged" them. They feel angry, deprived, and excluded. Because of slavery and other forms of racism, some blacks expect compensation is rightfully due to them. They seek special treatment and feel that society owes them something. They justify inappropriate behavior by considering it retribution for past oppression. The belief is that years of discrimination call for some retaliation. Clients experiencing this warning sign will probably be angry, have difficulty following rules, and constantly challenge authority.

Underlying Recovery Issues: Entitlement, rationalization, vengefulness, terminal uniqueness, anger, resentment, hypersensitivity, justification.

5. If you're black, get back.

This warning sign describes racism within the black culture. For years blacks have heard messages describing black as inferior. As a result many blacks have come to believe this to be true. Some blacks experience prejudice against their own people and dislike for their own black features. For example, they will see lighter skin and straighter hair as better than dark skin and kinky hair, often described as "bad" hair. They might prefer to do business with white companies because they believe them to be superior to black. Clients experiencing this warning sign will probably have low self-esteem and a dislike or disregard for other blacks. They may feel a white counselor will be better qualified.

Underlying Recovery Issues: Inadequacy, judgment, tunnel vision, prejudice, stereotyping, superiority complex, inferiority complex, confusion, shame, people-pleasing, and racism.

6. I have to work twice as hard just to be in the game.

This warning sign describes determination and desire to succeed gone wild. Many blacks feel they must work extra hard in order to overcome the obstacles placed in their life due to their race. They believe that as a black person you have to be twice as good just to get a chance. There is much pressure to succeed and prove themselves to their families and the world. They often feel as though they represent the whole black race. They perceive that their failure will portray blacks as incompetent. As a result of this need to succeed many blacks compromise their health and recovery for work. Clients experiencing this warning sign might frequently miss sessions, be competitive, have many stress-related physical problems, and be hypersensitive to criticism.

Underlying Recovery Issues: Overachievement, unrealistic expectations, pressure to perform, perfectionism, codependency, inadequacy, hypersensitivity to criticism, workaholism, compulsivity, victimization, distrust.

7. I'm only comfortable around my own people.

This warning sign describes exclusivity and distrust. Many blacks don't trust other people, especially people who are different than they are. They will resist getting into relationships with people they don't feel they have much in common with. They will frequently avoid relationships with whites, whom they distrust, and even with other blacks with whom they don't identify. They will gravitate to a small group of people they perceive to be like themselves and avoid most others. Clients experiencing this warning sign will be resistant to taking risks and will discount feedback from those they perceive to be unlike themselves.

Underlying Recovery Issues. Avoidance, discomfort, exclusion, focusing on differences rather than similarities, isolation, laziness, stagnation.

8. So what's wrong with being cool?

This warning sign describes a cultural identity based on street behaviors and attitudes. For many blacks being cool is a way of life. They have developed and nurtured their behavior often as a survival mechanism. The arrogance, defiance, and language stem from a need to identify, belong, and survive in what can be a harsh subculture. For many addicts the "street" lifestyle is as addictive as the drugs themselves. In this case the client has much invested in his persona and will fight to hold onto it. Clients experiencing this warning sign will be manipulative, resistant to change, and antagonistic.

Underlying Recovery Issues. Cockiness, discomfort in recovery, manipulation, narcissism, fear of change, justification, addiction to old lifestyle, intimidation.

9. I have been hurt by racism.

This warning sign describes the response of blacks being victimized by racism. Most blacks have at some time in their life been the victim of racism. The pain and discomfort blacks feel as a result of this racism is deep and lingering. Many blacks will not remain in a situation where they feel they have been victimized by someone's prejudice. This means many blacks have opted out of treatment and other recovery situations where they perceived they had experienced a racist act. Even though most blacks expect a certain amount of racism, they will not tolerate it for long. Clients experiencing this warning sign will be very depressed, angry, and disillusioned. They may shut down or want to abandon recovery.

Underlying Recovery Issues: Victimization, anger, resentment, self-pity, fear, disillusion, depression, cynicism, distrust.

10. I can be a racist, too.

This warning sign describes the process of blacks being the perpetrators of racism. There are many racist blacks who display the same kind of prejudice, discrimination, and bigotry as any other extremist group. They often feel justified in their racism and will report that it is a defense mechanism. They will see other races as the enemy. They will be abusive and act inappropriately in mixed-culture environments. Clients experiencing this warning sign will have difficulty interacting with nonblacks and blacks centered in white culture.

Underlying Recovery Issues: Racism, anger, vengefulness, exclusion, threatening others, intimidation, fear, isolation.

11. I like being the only black in the group.

This warning sign describes the "token black" syndrome. There are some blacks whose identity and self-esteem come from being accepted by nonblacks. They have found acceptance and inclusion in white society because of their race. They protect their role and tend to use it to their advantage.

They are opportunists who have found a way to gain access to otherwise off-limit situations and opportunities. In many cases they are accepted based on their race, not their merits as a person. They will allow themselves to be manipulated and sometimes ridiculed in order to reap the perceived benefits of the relationship. Clients experiencing this warning sign will be opportunistic and manipulative. They will gravitate toward nonblacks and might feel competitive toward other blacks.

Underlying Recovery Issues: Low self-esteem, codependency, shame, guilt, fear, dishonesty, self-doubt, neediness, feeling different, people-pleasing.

12. I knew it all along.

This warning sign describes the pessimism and distrust many blacks feel. Many blacks feel that most people are racist, so why bother with them. They have become jaded and cynical when it comes to having faith in other people. They have difficulty believing in nonblacks and are often disillusioned about life in general. They feel the need to always "watch their backs" and spend much of their time in a survival mode. Clients experiencing this warning sign will have a very small support system, which can be easily dismantled by their lack of trust.

Underlying Recovery Issues: Cynicism, paranoia, tunnel vision, hypersensitivity, distrust, pessimism, depression, guardedness, reservation, anger.

13. I shouldn't act too black.

This warning sign describes the shame many blacks feel about their blackness. I was told as a child to "act my age and not my color." This implies that acting black demonstrates my inferiority. Many blacks feel uncomfortable with their identity and attempt to minimize their blackness. They feel their race is second class, and so they tend to downplay their black characteristics. They make deliberate attempts to have their race be excused or ignored. They believe that "acting too black" is a sign of ignorance. It embarrasses them when they see other blacks using slang and acting out old stereotypes. Clients experiencing this warning sign will be apologetic and ashamed of their blackness. They may only "act black" when they are extremely uncomfortable or angry.

Underlying Recovery Issues: Shame, self-loathing, self-doubt, anger, resentment, depression, helplessness, frustration, confusion.

14. I don't stand up enough for my culture.

This warning sign describes a form of cultural codependency many blacks experience. Oftentimes blacks will avoid expressing their own cultural beliefs, behaviors, and attitudes for fear of making another culture uncomfortable. They will be aware of how their gatherings and actions can cause distress among their nonblack colleagues. Many blacks will engage in caretaking of their nonblack associates even at the cost of their own cultural needs. They might deprive themselves of an opportunity to express themselves culturally to avoid discomfort, confusion, and even ridicule from others. They are careful in the way they dress and behave around nonblacks, and often have resentment about the perceived need to conform. Clients experiencing this warning sign will be resentful, caretaking, and will often decline to discuss their true feelings.

Underlying Recovery Issues: Codependency, resentment, frustration, denial, control, internalizing, depression, projecting, shutting down, stuffing feelings.

15. My sexual behavior can sabotage my recovery.

This warning sign describes both sexual addiction and the act of confusing sex with love. There are many blacks who feel much pressure to perform sexually. There are myths that proclaim blacks to be superior lovers. Sex is one of the few arenas where blacks have a sense of being "better than" nonblacks. For those who believe this to be true, much of their self-esteem and self-worth comes from sex. Many use sex to fix, to medicate, and as a substitute for intimacy. Many experience such a lack of love in their lives that they confuse sex with love. They sometimes knowingly have sex with people for the illusion of love. Many blacks relapse as a result of sexual activities that are clearly not conducive to recovery. Clients who experience this warning sign will act out sexually in treatment and other recovery settings. They will resort to sexualizing when uncomfortable and they will resent being confronted about this behavior, because it is one of the only things that gives them self-worth.

Underlying Recovery Issues: Sexual addiction, substitution, low self-esteem, need, control, poor impulse control, slippery situations, obsessive thoughts, fantasizing, high-risk behavior, dishonesty, manipulation.

16. I'm working myself to death.

This warning sign describes trying to earn self-worth through work and material possessions. Many blacks have been taught that self-worth comes from what you have and do, not from who you are as a person. Many blacks view job titles and possessions as means to overcome a sense of inadequacy. They seek more and more possessions to prove to the world that they are valuable, worthwhile, and important human beings. The overall dissatisfaction with themselves and their life is often disguised with fancy clothes and cars. And because real self-worth doesn't come from property or prestige, they are never satisfied. Clients experiencing this warning sign will be braggarts, "name-droppers," cocky, and narcissistic. They will also be highly stressed and hypersensitive to criticism.

Underlying Recovery Issues: Workaholism, arrogance, substitution, pressure, inadequacy, pessimism, materialism, self-indulgence, low self-esteem, and greed.

17. I'm so angry.

This warning sign describes extreme difficulty managing anger. Many blacks who experience intense anger have difficulty expressing and managing this emotion. In the AA "Big Book" it refers to "justifiable resentment" as being dangerous for the alcoholic. In many cases the anger blacks feel is perceived to be justified and therefore more difficult to manage. They will often suppress the anger until they erupt in a possibly violent fit of rage. Many times they will be afraid of their rage and attempt to deny that they are angry. In some cases they grew up being taught that it was unsafe to express anger and they subsequently learn to "stuff" it. Sometimes people refer to "black rage" as blacks' response to years of discrimination. Many nonblacks get very uncomfortable when blacks get angry, and view it as threatening and inappropriate. This interpretation perpetuates blacks' difficulty expressing anger. Clients experiencing this warning sign may be seen as "stewing" or sulking, with a potential to explode. They will also feel frustrated by their inability to effectively and appropriately vent their anger. They may have fear about hurting themselves or others.

Underlying Recovery Issues: Rage, anger, depression, revenge, fear, self-destruction, obsession, frustration, victimization, justification.

18. Don't tell me what to do.

This warning sign describes difficulty with authority. Many blacks have a big problem with people telling them what to do. They resist authority and tend to have control issues. They historically don't trust others and don't feel safe when others are in control. They will act out and be defiant when put in a position where they don't have the power. They will attempt to engage in power struggles and have difficulty with the concept of surrender. Clients experiencing this warning sign will be resistant, argumentative, and fearful. They may attempt to undermine the treatment and/or recovery process for themselves and others.

Underlying Recovery Issues: Distrust, antagonism, power struggles, control issues, resistance, feeling unsafe, authority issues, resentment, fear, unable or unwilling to be vulnerable, paranoia.

19. I don't date other blacks.

This warning sign describes blacks who will not date other blacks because they believe them to be inferior. They will choose their partners primarily based on race. As long as they are not black they have a chance. Some blacks believe that by dating other races they are getting a better-quality partner. They believe that blacks are "less than," and so they seek dating partners from other races. This is a form of internal racism, which is probably a result of years of "black is bad and white is better" conditioning. Some blacks will overlook many flaws in their mate as long as they are the "right" race. They see their nonblack partners as boosts to their self-esteem. The partners are often flaunted and treated like trophies. Clients who experience this warning sign may be uncomfortable around blacks of the opposite sex. They tend to have a history of dysfunctional unfulfilling relationships.

Underlying Recovery Issues: Superiority, shame, guilt, resentment, judgment, low self-esteem, grandiosity, internal racism, exclusion.

20. I wish people weren't so afraid of me.

This warning sign describes the reaction to the fear of blackness. Blacks have frequently been portrayed as villains and dangers to white society. As a result many nonblacks are fearful of blacks, particularly black males. That fear is the basis for this warning sign. Many blacks experience fear and suspicion from other races even though they may have done nothing to provoke it. Oftentimes blacks will become resentful and disgusted when such a fearful reaction is perceived to be unwarranted. This causes much frustration and sadness for many blacks. Clients experiencing this warning sign may express deeply hurt feelings or resentment. They feel powerless to change others' reactions, which increases isolation and loneliness.

Underlying Recovery Issues: Anger, sadness, depression, resentment, exclusion, discomfort, fear, pessimism, loneliness, hopelessness, and helplessness.

21. I can't betray my family.

This warning sign describes family ties that threaten recovery. For some blacks the family bond is very strong, even in cases where the family is dysfunctional. Frequently blacks feel a strong sense of responsibility to their families even though the family relationship might jeopardize their recovery. Some have to choose between family and recovery. Many blacks have been unable to maintain recovery and simultaneously a relationship with certain family members. They will have much pressure and guilt when they attempt to separate from the family, and they may not survive in recovery. Clients experiencing this warning sign are torn between a sense of responsibility to their recovery and their family. They are confused by the conflicting messages they get from family members and their recovery support system.

Underlying Recovery Issues: Confusion, codependency, fear, depression, pressure, overresponsibility, internal conflict, powerlessness, anxiety, high-risk situations.

22. I have a spiritual dilemma.

This warning sign describes how spiritual conflicts become a threat to recovery. Some blacks who once felt close to God, now feel they have let God down. They have so much spiritual shame and guilt that they are unable to reconnect. They feel spiritually deficient and lack insight as to this area of their recovery. On the other hand, some blacks get so enmeshed in their pursuit of spirituality that they lose sight of their addiction. Many will seek refuge and recovery in the church. However, they lack a support system that understands and confronts their addiction. They might feel uncomfortable discussing their Higher Power in 12-Step meetings. They feel discouraged from getting too "religious," so they don't feel meetings are helping them. Clients experiencing this warning sign become stagnant in their recovery. They have difficulty completing the spiritual tasks of recovery. They might appear "holier than thou" or spiritually less than.

Underlying Recovery Issues: Shame, guilt, depression, hopelessness, despair, exclusivity, minimizing, inadequate support system, confusion, anger, resentment, spiritual confusion, people-pleasing, codependency, feeling different.

Chapter 13

The Seven Clinical Processes

In this chapter I will briefly describe the goals of the seven clinical processes developed by Terence T. Gorski. These processes are designed to assist clients in identifying and managing relapse warning signs and developing a schedule of activities that support continued recovery. The description I will offer will be only a small overview. I strongly suggest you acquire *Relapse Prevention Counseling Workbook* by Terence T. Gorski, which contains in-depth descriptions and clinical exercises for each process.

I also recommend you get training or work with a therapist trained in the CENAPS Model of Relapse Prevention Therapy. I suggest that the therapist has had training since October 1995 when CENAPS made significant changes in the model.*

The temptation for many clients and clinicians is to relax once the warning signs are identified. There is a profound sense of discovery that accompanies warning sign

---

*For a list of Certified Relapse Prevention Specialists in your area call CENAPS: 708/799-5000.

identification. Clients often feel enlightened and confident that now that they know what their warning signs are they are better prepared to avoid relapse. However, it has been my experience as well as that of many other relapse prevention specialists that if clients don't immediately identify effective management strategies for their warning signs they have a tendency to act them out. In other words, if there is too much delay between the time the warning sign is identified and a management strategy is put in place, there is potential for clients to relapse.

I have personally seen several clients demonstrate the same irrational thoughts and self-defeating behaviors that surfaced in their warning signs, while procrastinating on developing management strategies. The purpose of this work is to enhance recovery and avoid relapse, but if it is done improperly it can create more relapse issues. So get the training and get the literature; be prepared to use this model to its full potential—your client deserves that.

Process 1: Warning Sign Identification

The client will review either the Brief Warning Signs List or the original thirty-seven Relapse Warning Signs List developed by Terence T. Gorski, *and* review the twenty-two Relapse Warning Signs for African Americans. The client will identify relapse warning signs he has experienced and choose one to learn more about.

Process 2: Warning Sign Analysis

The client will analyze the selected warning sign by giving it a personal title and description. This title and description should be in the client's own words and easy to understand and remember. The client will then identify the irrational thoughts, unmanageable feelings, and self-defeating urges and actions that drive the relapse.

Process 3: Situation Mapping

The client will describe two situations that occurred in recovery where the selected warning sign was activated. The first situation will be one in which the warning sign was managed poorly. Here the client will identify self-defeating behaviors that drive the relapse process. The second situation will be one in which the warning sign was managed effectively, and here the client will begin to identify effective, recovery-based coping mechanisms.

Process 4: Thought Management

The client will learn to identify the "stinking thinking," cognitive distortions, and irrational thoughts that drive the selected relapse warning sign. The client will learn more effective ways of thinking that will help to avoid relapse and promote cognitive stability.

Process 5: Feeling Management

The client will learn to identify the unmanageable feelings that drive the selected relapse warning sign, and develop more effective ways of managing these feelings that will help to avoid relapse.

Process 6: Behavior and Situation Management

The client will learn to intervene in his own relapse process by identifying three intervention points in a high-risk situation. Clients will learn to use the situation map to plan intervention points where they can use more effective ways of thinking, feeling, and acting to avoid relapse.

Process 7: Recovery Planning

The client will develop a concrete, specific, and measurable schedule of recovery activities that will support the ongoing identification and management of relapse warning signs. This written recovery plan will address issues uncovered in the selected warning sign. The recovery plan will assure that the work the client does in recovery is specific to the problems the client faces in life.

A Challenge for You

As I'm writing this chapter it's been almost a year since I first wrote the Relapse Warning Signs for African Americans and the Guidelines for the Clinicians. During that time I have had the opportunity to participate in numerous field studies using these warning signs. I have also lectured at several workshops and seminars regarding cross-cultural counseling and relapse prevention. I have been overwhelmed with the support and enthusiasm that has been expressed to me.

Countless clinicians, both black and nonblack, have expressed to me that this work is much needed. I've been told that it appropriately deals with real and current issues in treatment today. Black clients have said to me that the warning signs have helped them to talk about difficult issues. They report that the list has created a forum for them to discuss what it's like to be black in recovery. By using the underlying recovery themes they are able to move out of the problem and into the solution.

Therapists have stated that the Guidelines for the Clinicians have empowered them to work more effectively with all minority clients. Many have found this section to be a useful tool to help them identify their own strengths and weaknesses. They feel that the suggestions are thought provoking and easy to understand. I was appreciative but surprised by the response I received.

This was my first attempt at writing. I didn't feel convinced that I could effectively put into words what I was thinking and feeling. I was concerned that it would be difficult to express all the emotions that surrounded many of the warning signs. I wondered if any of this would make sense to anyone other than myself. I didn't know if I had the time to see this thing through. But it all seemed to work itself out. There were many days that I watched in fascination as my fingers flew across the keyboard. I could hardly type fast enough to keep up with my ideas, and each time I reread something I found ways to make it clearer. And I had so much help.

I remember when I showed Terry Gorski the first draft. I anxiously awaited his feedback. He's published so many books, and has, in many ways, mentored me. I respect his opinion as a writer, a therapist, and a friend. Well, after a long pause he said to me, "This is good—but it can be great!"

He made some good suggestions about sentence structure and presupposition. He helped me to step back and really think about what I was trying to say. He wanted this to work, not just because his name was going on it, but because he thought it was important. I love him for that.

Sometimes I would be lying in bed and a thought would pop into my head. I'd rush down the hall to my computer and write it down. I'd see clients or people I know in recovery who would trigger a new warning sign and I'd write that down, too. I carried a notebook full of ideas around for months. But after a while I realized that I had finished with my part. It appeared that this was enough for now. I became ready to turn it over.

So now you have it. I hope this book found its way into the hands of someone who needed it, that it opened an eye or two, that it created a discussion that promoted healing, that someone got as much satisfaction out of reading it as I did out of writing it. But most of all I hope you realize this work is not done. This is not the end but the beginning. I challenge you to use what you've learned and build on it, to do what you can to bring recovery to the black community, to be more effective as a clinician working with any minority. And I challenge you to continue the dialogue. You may have valuable feedback and ideas about this model, and I encourage you to share them with Terry and me. Thanks and God bless.

If you have comments or suggestions, please feel free to write me: Roland Williams, c/o The CENAPS Corporation, 18650 Dixie Highway, Homewood, IL 60430.

Training and Consultation

Terence T. Gorski is available for personal and program consultation, lecturing, and clinical skills training workshops. He also routinely schedules workshops, executive briefings, and personal growth experiences for clinicians, program managers, and policymakers. He can be contacted at CENAPS (708) 799-5000.

TC '0